PRAYER

Bring
the Power of God
into Your Life

Other Books by Phil Batchelor

Raising Parents: Nine Powerful Principles

Love is a Verb: published by St Martins Press

The Purpose of Life: published by Danville International Publishing Company, LLC

Prayer

Bring
the Power of God
into Your Life

Phil Batchelor

Prayer: Bring the Power of God into Your Life:

Published by:
Danville Publishing Company
PO Box 3213
Danville, California 94526

ISBN 0-9748528-4-8
978-0-9748528-4-3

Library of Congress Control Number:
2006904112

Printed in the United States of America.

10 9 8 7 6 5 4 3 2 1

Dedicated to our
Heavenly Father
and
His Son Jesus Christ, our Savior

In Memory of
Roland Lynn

Acknowledgments

This book is a composite of true stories from the lives of many faithful men and women who graciously gave permission for their experiences to be shared in this volume.

I also express deep appreciation to Denise Mason and Sara Hoffman for substantial assistance in the editorial process; Melinda Batchelor and Tove Henn for their research assistance, to Steve Farrell for his inspired and insightful suggestions; and to David Freeman for his tireless assistance in the production of this volume. I also thank my dear wife, Carolee Batchelor, for help and support in making this book possible.

I thank Dave Christensen and Cheryl and Lauren Locey for their generous assistance and Jared Stone, Alan Johnson, Phil Andersen, Jeff Hart and the many other people who spent time reading drafts of the final manuscript and offering valuable suggestions.

CONTENTS

Introduction

Prayer

Bring the Power of God into Your Life

—•—

*P*eople of integrity have long known that there is a power higher than themselves and have sought for guidance from that power. Contained within the pages of this book are a few of the countless, wonderful experiences of how the God of Heaven has intervened to assist those who have asked for help in solving their problems, overcoming their weaknesses, and improving the overall quality of their lives.

The inspiring stories contained within the pages of this volume provide ample evidence that our incredible Creator is also a loving and caring Heavenly Father. His love and devotion are everywhere evident in the lives of ordinary men and women who have sought for divine intervention to lift and assist them.

As we study the teachings of Jesus Christ, the greatest person to ever walk the face of the earth, it will help us to understand how we should pray. The Savior not only teaches us what we should ask for, but he models for us the way to keep the channels of communication open with our Father in Heaven. He also helps us to recognize how answers to prayers are received and increases our understanding as to why some prayers are granted and others are not.

Receiving answers to our prayers should not be an occasional experience but should be a common daily occurrence that continually enriches, edifies, and guides us. There is no direction contained within the Bible that is as oft repeated as to knock, seek, ask, and pray. When we humble ourselves and call on our Heavenly Father for help he will open the windows of heaven and pour out a blessing there will not be room enough to receive.

Included in the faith-promoting stories of prayer chronicled in this volume are accounts of some great and noble men of history who humbled themselves to call on a power greater than themselves. Men such as George Washington, John Adams, Thomas Jefferson, Benjamin Franklin, Abraham Lincoln, and Sir Isaac Newton sought the blessings of heaven through prayer. We can only wonder how successful they would have been without the intervention of heaven in their lives. And well might we ask the same question of ourselves, "How will my life turn out if I continually invite the guidance of an all wise and all knowing God to guide me?"

14   Prayer

Chapter One

The Incredible Power of God

—•—

I remember that horrifying experience like it happened yesterday, yet it took place many years ago. We had just purchased a new house and were involved in the tedious task of putting in a new lawn as was Roland, a friend of ours who lived nearby.

Roland and I rented a trailer to get some sawdust to mix into the hard clay in our front yards. The sawmill was located up in the Santa Cruz Hills, only accessible from Highway 17, a steep, winding road that was treacherous and had been the scene of many accidents.

Roland hitched the trailer to his car and off we went. At the back of the mill a large front loader dumped two scoops of sawdust into the trailer. Then we started for home. Before we got on Highway 17, I suggested that we pull over for a prayer since we were worried about the steep grade. After praying for a safe return home, we started up the hill.

As the hill grew steeper, we could feel the tremendous pull of the trailer. We worried that it might come loose before we reached the summit. The large double trailer truck that was impatiently tailgating us heightened our anxiety. After what seemed like an eternity we finally reached the summit. We offered a silent prayer of thanks and then relaxed.

Little did we know that our troubles were just beginning? We did not realize that the trailer was greatly overloaded. When the scoop on the loader at the sawmill had gone back for the second scoop it was mostly saturated sawdust and wet mud instead of the lighter dry sawdust.

The trailer began to fishtail as we started down the steep and winding turns of Highway 17. Each turn in the road accelerated the whipping motion of the trailer. Soon it became so violent that it was forcing the car and trailer to swing back and forth across both lanes of the freeway.

We were terrified as we looked back and saw the huge semi truck bearing down on us. Suddenly Roland yelled, "The car is out of control!" There was nothing he could do to keep us from being propelled like a rocket towards the central steel guardrail of the freeway to what would be certain death. We braced for impact!

To our amazement the impact never came. We stopped inches from the guardrail. The huge truck behind us somehow managed to stop before it ran over us.

We were trembling as we got out of the car to survey the damage. The car and trailer were straddled across both lanes and so completely closed the road down that the only way the Highway Patrol and the tow truck could reach us was by coming up the wrong way on the freeway.

When we examined the trailer more closely we discovered why we were not killed that frightful day. The back axle of the trailer was broken in half, as if a giant hand had pushed the trailer to the ground, instantly immobilizing it just inches from the guard rail.

A tow truck pulled the trailer off to the side of the road, leaving the car virtually unscarred. We drove home, thanking God for saving our lives and pondering on the words of the prayer we had previously offered asking for protection and safety.

This situation, where an out of control car and trailer were miraculously immobilized and a huge semi truck was stopped in its tracks, reinforced my awareness of the tremendous power that God has available to bless and protect us.

The Incredible Creator

Have you ever taken time to ponder the power of God and his ability to accomplish so many things? Consider for a moment some of the things that he has done.

Gazing into the evening sky on a dark, star-studded night can help us to see the grandeur of God's creations and what he is capable of doing. In this regard the Psalmist of the Old Testament, records, *"He [God] telleth the number of the stars; he calleth them all by their names. Great is our Lord, and of great power: his understanding is infinite."* [1]

We may ask ourselves, "How big is this universe in which we live?" I received the slightest hint of just how large the universe really is when I recently read a press release from the National Aeronautics and Space Administration (NASA). NASA reported that they have been exploring the vastness of the universe with the help of the Hubble Space Telescope, and that an international team of astronomers has discovered a galaxy an estimated 13 billion light years away from earth. [2]

In order to determine how far from the earth this galaxy is, you would have to multiply the distance light travels in one year, (5.8 trillion miles), times the number of years, (13 billion) you would have to travel at the speed of light. It is an almost inconceivable distance.

This measurement would only determine how far we can see into the universe from the earth. Who knows if even this tremendous distance is a beginning to the vastness of the universe? Nevertheless the vastness of space, any way you measure it, is beyond our comprehension. It is truly humbling to contemplate the universe or the hundreds of millions of solar systems, suns, and planets that are a part of it.

I think it is even more daunting to try and understand the Supreme Creator who ordered and organized these countless celestial bodies, a God with such marvelous power that it is beyond our ability to comprehend him. Although we cannot begin to understand the majesty of God, we can examine the intricacies of the earth upon which we reside; and, in doing so, quickly see that God pays careful attention to even the smallest details.

This earth is in a carefully prescribed orbit as it revolves around the sun and moves through space. Its distance from the sun gives it just enough light and heat to sustain human life. If it were to stray just a little too close or too far from the sun, it would be consumed by fire or become a ball of ice. It is tilted on its axis at just the right angle to create the seasons, and it rotates to bring the necessary intervals of light and darkness. Life on earth operates under the most amazing system of checks and balances, allowing it to perpetuate itself.

When I examine the perfection and workmanship of God's hand, I am reminded of the statement by

Ralph Waldo Emerson, who said, *"All I have seen teaches me to trust the Creator for all I have not seen."* [3]

I believe that if God is so attentive to the details of his creations, then certainly he must also be concerned about the details of our lives. The evidence that he does intervene in our lives, if we *invite* him, is so overwhelming that it would be impossible to chronicle the countless experiences of people whose lives have been blessed by prayer.

I think if we knew even a few of the endless number of instances of people's prayers being answered it might increase our faith that the wonderful power God possesses can also be brought into our lives if we will ask for it.

Prayer is perhaps the greatest unused resource in the world. It can help us solve even the most difficult problems. The story that follows is one account of a young mother who reached for the power of heaven.

Sentenced to Death

A number of years ago Kari, her husband, and their two children took passage on a ship that sailed from Norway to America. Once they arrived in New York City they traveled to San Francisco, California where they rented a very humble room in the red light district. Within a few days, Kari's husband took a job on a freighter and sailed away, leaving Kari and her children to fend for themselves.

Kari was in trouble. She had no money, could not speak the language, and could not even find anyone who could understand her. Soon she and the children were out on the street and desperately going from one relief organization to another seeking help. She felt so lonely and helpless since there was no one she could talk to. Finally the Salvation Army came to her rescue and helped them with some money, food, and clothing.

In time, Kari obtained a job as a live-in housekeeper watching two children for a female physician who lived in Piedmont, California. However, when she found that this woman was drugging her children to keep them quiet, and wanted to do the same to Kari's children, she moved into an inexpensive apartment in a very poor area in Richmond, California. They had very little money and survived by eating a lot of potatoes. In fact, her daughter, Tove, indicated that is all she could remember eating in those days."

Then one day while she was crossing the street Kari lost consciousness and was rushed to a hospital in San Francisco.

Tests were performed and the news was not good. The doctor said, "I am very sorry to tell you this but you have cancer! And it is so far advanced that it is intertwined around your spine to the point that we cannot remove it with surgery. You need to go home and set your affairs in order and find someone to raise your children because you only have about six months left to live."

She questioned, "Why, why did this have to happen to me? Don't I have enough burdens as a single parent struggling to raise my children in a foreign country? Haven't I lived a good life and tried to do what is right? It just isn't fair!"

During the next few days she was very emotional. She intermittently had feelings of anger, fear, resentment, and depression. This brave young mother felt helpless as she agonized and suffered from loneliness. She wondered, who would raise her children? Who would love them and care for them, dry their tears and bandage up their cuts and scrapes and tuck them into bed at night the way she did?

She suffered through days of mental anguish, homesickness, and worry. Then, one day after vomiting all the way home during the bus ride from San Francisco where she visited the doctor's office, something happened inside of Kari. She knew she could not go on this way any longer and decided to turn to God for help.

She knelt down by her window that evening and began to pray as she had done many times before. But this time something was different. She confided in her Father in Heaven that she was not going to take any more medication or participate in the medical treatment that had made her so ill. Then she pleaded, "Heavenly Father, I cannot do this any longer by myself. I am turning my life, what there is left of it, over to you. If you want me to live and raise my children, then bless me that I will be able to do it. But if you want me to die, that is okay also. I will do whatever you want me to do."

When Kari finished praying she felt a sense of peace come over her and a feeling that one way or another everything would be okay. She no longer felt alone. God had heard her petitions and she had placed her life in his hands.

What happened next was truly astonishing. The doctors were shocked and could not explain it, but her cancer completely disappeared.

Not only did this faithful lady live to see her children grow to maturity, but she also has grandchildren who have grown to adulthood. Now in her eighties, she is a witness that without God's intervention in her life, she would have died, for there was nothing man could have done to save her.

Overcoming Impossible Odds

You might ask, "Is there any challenge we might encounter that is too difficult for God to help us overcome?" This was answered in a dramatic way by a story found in the book of Judges in the Old Testament of the Bible.

The children of Israel, due to their lack of obedience to God, were in captivity to a group of people known as the Midianites. When things became intolerable for the Israelites, after years of being in captivity, they prayed to God for relief.

God answered their prayers in a most unusual way. First, he called a lowly wheat farmer named Gideon to lead them out of captivity. And although Gideon protested, "... *my family is poor in Manasseh, and I am the least in my father's house,*" [4] he responded to the call.

Gideon raised up an army of 32,000 men to face the enormous Midianite army and their allies, the Amalekites, that the Bible tells us were "... *like grasshoppers for multitude; and their camels were without number, as the sand by the sea side for multitude.*" [5]

Next, God had Gideon reduce his already hopelessly outnumbered army from 32,000 down to 300 soldiers. It was important for God to teach these faithless and disobedient people to know that it was by his divine power that they would be saved from their enemies, not their own cunning and strength.

Gideon's tiny army followed the strategy that was laid out by the Lord, and with the help of God, these 300 soldiers miraculously defeated their enemies. This incredible conquest was proof to even the most hard-hearted, skeptical, and doubting person that this victory could never have been accomplished without God's intervention.

This wonderful account reminds us that regardless of the size or magnitude of the problem we may face, there is no foe, challenge, or obstacle we will encounter in life that is too difficult for us to overcome if God is willing to assist us. Once we come to understand this important fact, then our focus can shift to doing all within our power to draw closer to God.

26   Prayer

Chapter Two

A Cosmic Creator, a Loving Father

—•—

*G*od may have the power to answer prayers, but how often will he take the time from his busy schedule of operating the universe to help us? How important must our need be before he will intercede and send help?

I am reminded of an experience that took place some years ago that involved two four-year-old girls named Denise and Melinda who had the childlike faith to call upon God for help in a time of need. This is their story as related by Melinda.

Lost But Not Alone

"When we were four years old, my twin sister, Denise, and I accompanied our mother to Montgomery Ward. As she went to the fitting rooms to try on some clothes, we were expressly told to stay right outside the door until she came out. Despite her explicit instructions, the draw of the escalator was too much for us—we snuck off to find adventure there. After spending what seemed like an hour playing on the escalator but was probably closer to 10 or 15 minutes, we decided we should probably go back to find Mom.

"We returned to the fitting room area where we believed her to be, peeking under the doors of the fitting room in four-year-old fashion to try to find her. None of the pairs of legs seen under the dressing room doors appeared to belong to our mother, so naturally we panicked.

We rushed to the nearest exit doors, not understanding at our young age that there are numerous exits from a large department store. We went outside to look for our big yellow station wagon—pretty hard to miss if you are actually looking in the right parking lot.

Unfortunately we were not looking in the right parking lot, so naturally we did not see our station wagon. When we couldn't find it, we concluded that our mother had forgotten about her four-year-old twin daughters and had driven home without us. We were very sad that we had been so easily forgotten.

"At this point we decided to ask Heavenly Father for help. We found a place behind a wall where the department store's dumpsters were kept, and there we knelt down and said a prayer. Then we got back on our feet and decided to walk the several miles back to our home. Off we went, leaving the store behind and heading out of the parking lot toward the street that led back to our home.

"Somehow, despite our 4-year-old innocence and ignorance, we walked in the right direction for probably a couple of hours, until we were within a mile or so of our home. At this point my sister Denise and I no longer agreed on which direction we needed to go. She thought we should go right while I was sure we needed to go left. After arguing for several minutes, we each went our separate ways. To make matters worse, it began to rain.

"Denise wandered several blocks until she reached a park, where she then realized she had gone the wrong way. Being alone and frightened, not to mention soaked to the skin, and having no idea what to do, she went and sat down on a park bench. Some teenage boys who were playing soccer nearby approached her to see if she needed any help when suddenly a car pulled up with two young women in it. They told the boys they would take care of her. After taking Denise to their home to get some dry clothes, the young ladies questioned her and found that she had "been left" by her mother at the store. Knowing this was very unlikely, they put Denise back in the car and set out to find the store where she had been left. Denise only knew that she had been at "the big store," which was not extremely helpful for the women trying to help her. So they drove along asking, "Is that the store?" until they reached the shopping mall that contained Montgomery Ward. The mall was so far from where they had found Denise that they couldn't believe it when she finally said, "That's it!" They took her to the mall's security office, where Denise was thrilled to receive a big bag of jelly beans while the security officer called her by-then frantic mother, who thought her daughters had been kidnapped. How relieved she must have been to have Denise back! But where was Melinda?

"Having chosen the correct path that would lead me home, I (Melinda) walked several blocks, certain that I knew exactly where I was and that I would be home soon. However, upon reaching a major intersection, I pushed the button that would tell me when I could cross the busy street. I stood there for what seemed like an eternity, but the walk signal never came.

It only showed the red hand meaning 'don't walk' and never actually changed to the green walk signal. Perplexed, I looked at all the cars rushing by and knew that I could never make it across this street without the help of the little green man at the crosswalk. So I just stood there in the rain wishing I was wearing more than my red sweater with the broken zipper.

"Then I noticed that a car had pulled over nearby. A woman from the car asked me if I was lost, but I knew better than to speak to strangers. So I dutifully ignored this woman . . . this stranger. I just looked straight ahead, pretending that I didn't hear the woman but feeling more and more anxious with each passing moment.

Then before I knew what was happening, the woman got out of the car, picked me up, and got back in the car. This woman and the man driving the car introduced themselves and said they wanted to help. Their names were Pat and Jim, and as I sat in the warm car, wrapped up in Pat's sweater, I somehow sensed that these people weren't going to hurt me, that I was now safe. So I finally answered their questions. I gave them my address, and Jim pulled out a roadmap of the city with which they were able to locate my street and then drive me home.

Shortly thereafter, my dad, who had been contacted earlier by Mom, arrived home and found me there. He immediately called the department store to give the happy news to Mom and to the police who had been called in by this time.

"As I look back on this day, it is so clear to me that the Lord heard and answered our prayer. It is truly a miracle that we both returned home safely. I am so grateful that Heavenly Father cared enough about two little girls to protect us from the world's many dangers and to send good people to us."

What is God Like?

You may ask, "How can I have the kind of faith these two little girls had, when I do not really know God?" You may acknowledge that there is a great and powerful cosmic Creator, who has set countless heavenly bodies in their orbits, but what has he to do with you? How can you have the faith to believe that God even cares about you, let alone that he will answer your prayers?

How do you find out what God is like? Is he, as some believe, the kind of being that has a thunderous voice, that breathes our threats, destruction, and condemnation and is severe, strict, harsh, unmerciful, unfeeling, and without love? We can find the answer to these questions if we turn to the Bible. In what is perhaps the most quoted verse from the Bible we learn, *"For God so loved the world, that he gave his only begotten Son, that whosoever believeth in him should not perish, but have everlasting life."*[6]

God sent Jesus Christ to Earth to serve as our Savior, to teach us, and to show us the things we should do. He was a perfect role model. One of the most important things that Jesus did was to teach us about God. He did this by the things he said and by living his life in a way that modeled the attributes of God.

In the fourteenth chapter of John we can read the account of Jesus teaching his apostles about God: *"If ye had known me, ye should have known my Father also..."*[7]

Then to further emphasize this point, Jesus responds to a question posed by Philip, one of the twelve apostles, who asks the Savior to show them God. The Savior tells him that those who have seen the Son have seen the Father; in other words, if the Father were present, he would conduct himself in exactly the same manner as Jesus did.

Later, when Jesus was responding to the questions of the people, he explained that he only did those things that his Father wanted him to do: *"Verily, verily, I say unto you, The Son can do nothing of himself, but what he seeth the Father do: for what things soever he doeth, these also doeth the Son likewise. For the Father loveth the Son, and sheweth him **all** things that himself doeth..."*[8]

In the third chapter of Hebrews, the Apostle Paul adds to our understanding of what God is like by telling us that Jesus Christ was created in the *"express image"* of his Father.[9]

Therefore, if you want to know about the Father, study the life, teachings, and character of the Son. Then you will come to know what God is like. If Jesus were tender and loving and devoted his life to serving, healing, helping, lifting, and teaching the people, what would we expect God to be like? He would be exactly the same. If this is true, and I believe it is, then what might God do if we pray and ask for help? Remember what God did when those two little girls knelt in the parking lot and asked him for help?

I know from personal experience that God hears the prayer of faith and responds. Last year I took my seven-year-old daughter, Hailey, to San Francisco as a special treat. We looked at the decorations in the store windows, rode on a cable car, shopped at the Disney store and ate dinner at a restaurant. After dinner we returned to our hotel room and watched a movie on television.

When it was time to go to sleep, the noises of a big city and the sirens piercing the night air frightened her and she snuggled up next to me. She lay there for some time, but could not fall asleep. Finally, she sat up in bed and said, "Daddy, will you ask Heavenly Father to help me fall asleep?" We knelt down and asked our Father in Heaven to help her fall sleep. Then she got back into bed and immediately fell asleep.

It should not be difficult for us to understand that God loves children and has great compassion for them and will answer the prayers of a small, frightened child. It was God whom Jesus was emulating when he said to his disciples, "*Suffer the little children to come unto me and forbid them not: for of such is the kingdom of God.*"[10]

What else do we know about Jesus Christ that will help us to understand more about God? The Savior was not only compassionate but was also perfect in every way. He was perfectly kind, loving, honest, tender, caring, fair, just, merciful, etc. Therefore, we can be assured that God has these same characteristics.

We must remember that it was the Father who was the role model for the Son, who then served as our role model.

God the Father is truly the kind of being that we can admire and revere. Once we come to understand that he is perfect, it is easier for us to have faith in him, to know he will never fail us or harm us. We can have confidence in him and know that he will never make a mistake.

I believe that our loving and caring God is perfectly mindful of us. The Savior taught us that not even a sparrow can fall to the ground without God's notice and that the hairs of our head are numbered to him whom we call our "Father." Matthew records Jesus Christ's words, *"Are not two sparrows sold for a farthing? And one of them shall not fall on the ground without your Father. But the very hairs of your head are all numbered. Fear ye not therefore, ye are of more value than many sparrows."*[11]

Yes, I know that God is mindful of all his creations, but I think he is particularly mindful of we who are his children.

C. S. Lewis said, *"[God] has infinite attention to spare for each one of us. He does not have to deal with us in the mass. You are as much alone with Him as if you were the only being He had ever created."* [12]

As the Psalmist put it, *"What is man that thou art mindful of him? And the son of man, that thou visitest him? For thou hast made him a little lower than the angels, and hast crowned him with glory and honour."*[13]

God is a perfect parent and he has asked us to call him Father, or Heavenly Father. He has created us in his own image and likeness as recorded in the first chapter of Genesis: *"And God said, Let us make man in our image, after our likeness: . . . So God created man in his own image, in the image of God created he him; male and female created he them."*[14]

Is God Happy to Hear From You?

Our Father in Heaven, who created us in his image and of whom Christ was in the "express image," is a tangible being who is totally approachable and welcoming.

I am reminded of an experience that was shared with me by a friend of mine named Spence, who is a physician. He said, "When I grew up and left home, I would often call my parents. When my father answered the phone, he would say, 'Hello son, how are you doing?' in a loud and enthusiastic way. I always felt he was happy and excited to hear from me and that he was proud of me. I knew if I had a problem or a concern that I was always welcome to call him and he would help me if he could, and I always felt better after talking with him."

Spence continued, "When I pray, I am reminded of this experience. I think as I address my Heavenly Father that he is always glad to hear from me and receives me in the same kind and enthusiastic way that my earthly father did. I feel like my Father in Heaven says, 'Well, hello my son, I am glad you called, it is nice to hear from you.' I believe he genuinely cares about me and is glad to hear from me and loves me. In fact, the greatest benefit I receive from prayer is not in being able to ask for things but is in the relationship I am able to establish with my Heavenly Father.

"This relationship gives me greater confidence that I can take on the challenges of life, and it makes me feel more secure and better about myself."

This same feeling, that Heavenly Father is a kind and loving Mentor who really cares about us, is one that little children who are humble and faithful are especially able to sense. Such was the case of a little five-year-old girl who lived in a rural area of Norway near the Fjords. Each day her father insisted that she go through the dark and heavily wooded area near their house to the main road to pick up the mail. But she was afraid to walk through the forested area by herself. So she prayed to her Heavenly Father and asked Him to help her.

As it is with all sincere, faithful prayers, God answered her. The thought came to her to find a stick that she could take with her every time she had to walk through the woods. This was not to be any ordinary stick, but a very special one. She believed that whenever she had this stick with her, Heavenly Father would take the other end of it and together they would go and get the mail. This special stick was kept just outside the back door of their house and provided great comfort to this tender little girl in her many trips through the frightening dark forest because she felt Heavenly Father's presence beside her.

We can discover that our Father in Heaven will also help us as we walk through the "frightening dark forests" of our life.

Do You Love God?

I believe that Heavenly Father is willing to help any of us if we will learn to love him and call upon him. Both the Old and New Testaments of the Bible declare, *"The first of all the commandments is . . . thou shalt love the Lord thy God with all thy heart, and with all thy soul, and with all thy mind, and with all thy strength: this is the first [and great] commandment."*[15]

When I was young I wondered why God, who is concerned about the operation of countless galaxies and solar systems, wants us to love him. But as I matured, it became evident that God does not need our love as much as we need to love him. When we learn to draw closer to our Heavenly Father and love him, we will place greater trust in him, will be more willing to confide our most intimate thoughts and feelings with him and have confidence that he will not harm us but will love and help us.

In time we will come to understand that what he wants for us is even greater than what we want for ourselves, and if we are willing to trust in our Heavenly Father, he will help us to have a more fulfilling and successful life. As a perfect parent our Father in Heaven wants only that which will best help his children, and I believe he waits for us with open arms to nurture and love us and to answer our prayers.

A friend of mine named Steve once told me of an experience from his childhood that helped him to obtain a better understanding of his Heavenly Father. It was a father/son camping trip that he took when he was about 12 years old. After his scout troop had hiked a long way, they stopped at a lake to do some fishing. But it did not take long for these young scouts to get bored and decide to explore. They climbed the rocks and cliff above the lake and soon found themselves high above the water. They climbed so high that they were barely able to see their fathers at the campsite below.

The boys lost track of time, and the appointed hour when they were supposed to be back at the lake had come and gone. When they finally realized what time it was, they were a long way from the lake. It took them some time to climb down the cliff, and when they finally reached the lake, the anxious fathers happily greeted their sons. All the fathers, that is, except Steve's.

Steve asked, "Where is my dad?" One of the fathers said, "He went out to look for you." So Steve started back out on the trail to try and find his dad.

Soon he spotted his father, who had climbed to the top of the cliff and was calling his name. Steve hurried along the trail, anxious to meet his father; but as he thought about it, he wondered about what his father would say. His father was a big and powerful man. Would his father be angry with him? Would he yell at him? Would he want to spank him? The more he thought about it, the more Steve began to worry.

Finally, as he rounded a curve in the trail Steve saw his father coming toward him with his great arms outstretched and tears in his eyes as he expressed his love for his son. Perhaps when we do meet our Heavenly Father, he will embrace us and express his love for us in much the same way that Steve's earthly father did so many years ago.

I believe that our loving Heavenly Father is most willing to bless us and has invited us to call upon him, but we must take the initiative to ask. The seventh chapter of Matthew records part of the Savior's marvelous discourse known as the Sermon on the Mount. In it Jesus teaches us that our Heavenly Father is waiting to answer our prayers and is able to bless us far more than even the most nurturing earthly parents.

"Ask, and it shall be given you; seek and ye shall find; knock, and it shall be opened unto you: For every one that asketh receiveth; and to him that knocketh it shall be opened. Or what man is there of you, whom if his son ask bread, will he give him a stone? Or if he ask a fish, will he give him a serpent? If ye then, being evil, know how to give good gifts unto your children, how much more shall your Father which is in heaven give good things to them that ask him?"[16]

If we as imperfect parents want to help our children and do what is best for them, then Heavenly Father, as a perfect Parent, is willing and able to do so much more for his children, if we will ask for his assistance. How marvelous it is to be a child of God!

We come to understand the loving nature of our Heavenly Father by studying the life of our beloved Savior, who is exactly like him. We do this by reading the scriptures, by living the commandments that are given to us in the Bible, and by regularly communicating with our Father in Heaven. The more we learn of the Son, the more we will be willing to trust in the Father and go to him to express our love and appreciation for the things he gives us each day. We will also develop confidence that we can ask him at any time, in any place, to help us or other people. And we can know that, if our prayers are sincere, our Heavenly Father will hear them.

42   Prayer

Chapter Three

Learning to Pray to Our Father in Heaven

———••———

o you have a desire to pray but are not sure how to effectively communicate with your Father in Heaven? Maybe you have wondered if your prayers ever do any good, or questioned if you are praying the way Heavenly Father wants you to pray.

I believe that there is a pattern to prayer that can help us to more effectively organize our thoughts and help us to gain greater confidence as we approach our Father in Heaven in prayer. Nevertheless, I think prayer is more about sincerity, honesty, humility, and faith than it is about form, pattern, or style.

A friend of mine named Satu shared the following very special story with me:

"It was in the spring of the year when my family had an experience we will never forget. Josh was a toddler at the time and was at the curious, adventurous age where he began to be interested in toys with wheels that he could ride. He had recently discovered a Little Tykes van that both he and his brother, Matt, spent hours sitting in and pushing each other around in.

"The rule was that the van stayed in the backyard because it was not safe to ride it in the front yard as our house was situated in a tree-covered lot with a very long and steep driveway. The end of the driveway connected to a narrow road, and beyond the road was a steep cliff with no visible bottom.

"I was in the garage trying to organize the clutter, and Matt and Josh were in the garage playing with each other. When I dropped a canning jar on the concrete floor and shattered it, I went to get a dustpan and broom to sweep it up. As I did I heard a strange sound coming from outside.

"It took about 10 seconds for my mind to register that I was hearing the sound of the Little Tykes van rolling down our long driveway. I quickly turned toward the sound and saw Joshua inside the van rapidly rolling down the driveway towards the road and cliff beyond.

"I began to run after the rapidly accelerating van that was carrying my precious little son, Josh. Instinctively, as a nurse trained in emergency situations, I yelled to Matt "Call 911!" and then offered these words of prayer, 'Heavenly Father, send your angels!'

"I followed the van over the cliff by getting down on my bottom and sliding down the steep cliff. From the top of the cliff, I could not see the van or Josh because of the sharp drop-off. I still remember that moment when my heart jumped for joy when I heard him crying and knew that he had survived.

"Following the sound, I saw Josh miraculously wedged between a fallen tree branch and the side of the hill, in the only safe spot that I could see. The van was nowhere to be seen. Later we found it completely ruined at the bottom of the hill with its door ripped off. The ambulance arrived and the paramedics strapped my son tightly to a board to keep him absolutely still in case of back or neck injuries, and I rode with him to the hospital.

"During the trip to the hospital, I felt the peace that comes only from the Lord and knew that Josh would be just fine. After several hours of testing we were told that Josh would be okay. He had not suffered any harm except for a few facial scratches.

"Heavenly Father heard my prayer and sent angels to save my son from this perilous situation because he is a kind and caring Parent."

This faithful mother uttered a five-word prayer as she was sliding down a driveway and scampering over a cliff, and Heavenly Father instantly heard and answered her urgent call for help.

I do not believe that we always need to find a private place where we can kneel down with our arms folded and our eyes closed in order to pray to our Father in Heaven. We can offer prayers at any time and in any place, whether kneeling beside our bed, driving down the road, hiking along a trail, or in a moment of crisis. Different situations call for different types of prayers. Any and all are acceptable to our Heavenly Father if they are sincere, offered in faith, and asking for those things that are right. I think he has heard every sincere, heartfelt prayer that has ever been offered.

However, you may ask, "Is there a way I can organize my thoughts, feelings and words in a way that will make my prayers more meaningful?" Perhaps the following series of questions and answers may help address this inquiry.

What is Prayer?

Prayer is a form of work that is designed to bring us closer to our Father in Heaven. Prayer requires effort. It is the process of bringing the mind of the petitioner into harmony with the mind of God. The object of prayer should not be to change the mind of our Heavenly Father but to ask for those favors and blessings he is already willing to grant to us and others if we will ask for them. As Soren Kierkegaard put it, "Prayer does not change God, but it changes him who prays."

When Should I Pray?

It is a good idea to pray every morning and ask Heavenly Father to help you in all that you are to do during the day, with special mention being made of any challenges facing you or someone else you are concerned about.

At the end of the day, it is a good practice to report to your Father in Heaven on how you have done during the day and to thank him for his help.

Besides personal prayers, some families have a family prayer both morning and evening to unite the family members and to reinforce the support and love of the family as a whole and in each member's life. On a daily basis, members of the family may take turns being the voice that offers the prayer.

Many people give thanks for the food they are to eat before they begin each meal.

Other than these prescribed times, we should feel free to pray whenever we want to talk to our Heavenly Father.

To borrow from a quotation about patriotism given by Adlai Stevenson, we might say prayer should not just constitute occasional "short, frenzied outbursts of emotion, but [should continue as] the tranquil and steady dedication of a lifetime."

How Often Should I Pray?

There is no prescribed number of times we should pray during the day. However, we might consider how often we would want to talk to the most loving and intelligent being in the universe if he were always readily available to us.

Recently I was talking to a group of teenagers about prayer, and I asked them how often they prayed during the day. One young man named Steve answered, "I pray between 30 and 35 times a day."

This sentiment was reinforced in a talk I heard in church given by a 17-year-old young lady named Abby, who said, "I am so glad that Father in Heaven does not place a quota on the number of times we can pray to him each day." Not only does God not place a quota on the number of times we can pray, but the Savior counsels us to *"pray always."*[17]

Many wise couples who have had long and happy marriages indicate that they kneel together before retiring to bed at night and pray to their Heavenly Father, often expressing appreciation and love for each other. It is difficult for an argument to carry over to the next day if you have knelt and prayed together the night before.

How Long Should I Pray?

We need to pray long enough to establish an open channel of communication with our Father in Heaven so we can give thanks, express our love, and request assistance if needed. Then we need to pause and wait for any feelings or thoughts that may come into our heart or mind in answer to our prayers.

The length of our prayers will vary depending on what we are praying for and the importance of our petitions. Some prayers may be offered silently just seconds before we are to undertake some important task, or may last for an extended length of time if we need to pour out our heart to our Father in Heaven in the privacy of our own room.

The Lord tells us that we are not to multiply many words, to use flowery language, to be praying to be seen (or heard) of men, or to use *"vain repetitions."*[18]

Where Should I Pray?

We should pray in the privacy of our homes both morning and evening. It is also perfectly appropriate to pray silently, anytime and in any place, when we need assistance or want to express our thanks to our Heavenly Father.

I have prayed while driving down the road, sitting in a meeting, at work preparing to face a serious challenge, heading for the emergency room of the hospital, walking on a mountain trail, sitting in a park, in a private setting listening to someone who is in need of help, standing in front of a room full of people, and in many other places.

What Should I Pray For?

It is appropriate to pray to express the desires of our heart to our loving and attentive Heavenly Father. We may pray to share the intimate concerns and feelings of our heart, such as when we are depressed, lonely, unloved, worried, afraid, nervous, confused, perplexed, overburdened and feeling unable to go on, or any other of a myriad of challenging situations in which we may find ourselves.

On the other hand, we may also want to express the joy and delight we find in life and to thank our kind and generous Heavenly Father for any of the countless ways he has blessed us: for the beautiful world, the food we have to eat, our friends and family, our health, the privilege of being able to pray, and for the Savior, Jesus Christ, and the fact that he has suffered for our sins and overcome death to allow us to be resurrected.

The apostle Paul counsels us to *"[Give] thanks always for all things unto God."*[19] If we take this literally, we should even be thankful for our trials and challenges because they can help strengthen and refine us, teach us humility, and remind us of our dependence upon God.

It is appropriate to pray and ask for assistance in anything we may need in life. We can pray for our health, our family, friends, enemies, the leaders of our country, the needy, our relationships, assistance in our jobs or for help to overcome challenges or problems. We should also pray to ask for forgiveness for the things we do wrong.

All of us will need to make many important decisions during our lifetimes when it would be helpful to have greater insight, understanding or wisdom. James counsels us to pray for wisdom: *"If any of you lack wisdom, let him ask of God, that giveth to all men liberally, and upbraideth not and it shall be given him."*[20]

We might also recognize that our Father in Heaven knows the things we need better than we do. As Jesus Christ tells us,"*…for your Father knoweth what things ye have need of, before ye ask him.*"[21] Therefore, it may be advisable to pray for the wisdom to know what to ask for in prayer.

I have found the only thing in life I can do more effectively without God's help is sin.

How Should I Pray?

Before you begin to speak, it may be helpful to remember that you are praying to your Father in Heaven. He is a kind and loving Father, who is a tangible being that cares about you, wants to hear from you, and wants to help you.

If the opportunity avails itself and you are alone in your bedroom, you may want to kneel beside your bed, close your eyes, concentrate on whom you are talking to and what you are saying, and keep your mind from wandering. You should speak from your heart when you talk to Heavenly Father and not use memorized prayers.

You need to pour out the feelings of your heart and tell him what you are thinking and feeling in the way you would talk to a beloved parent.

There is no special formula that has to be followed in order for God to answer your prayers. Although it is important for your prayers to be reverent and in good taste, you are not required to follow any pattern other than to pray from your heart with sincerity and genuineness. However, to more effectively be able to express yourself, it may be helpful to organize your thoughts and feelings in the following manner:

Step One: Address Heavenly Father

The first thing we need to do in offering a prayer is to address our Heavenly Father. If we follow the pattern of prayer given to us by the Savior, we will also show reverence for him as follows: *"Our Father which art in heaven, Hallowed be thy name."*[22]

Heavenly Father asks us to pray to him directly; he does not want us to go through anyone else. He employs no assistants, secretaries, or aides.

We do not need to make an appointment to talk to our Father in Heaven. We can pray anytime we want to talk to him.

Step Two: Give Thanks

Before we begin to list off the things we need or want Heavenly Father to do for us, we need to have the good manners to thank him for the things he has already given us.

The apostle Paul instructors us to, *"Pray without ceasing. In every thing* **give thanks***: for this is the will of God…"*[23]

When we express gratitude, it humbles us and helps us to have the proper attitude as we address our Father in Heaven.

Sometimes it is even appropriate to dedicate our entire prayer to the giving of thanks, without asking for anything else.

I remember hearing the story of a man who was so humble when he prayed that some individuals who heard him opened their eyes to see if Heavenly Father was standing there in his presence. This man devoted the majority of his prayers to thanking God.

Step Three: Ask for Help

In the Bible, we are repeatedly instructed to ask our Father in Heaven for those things we have need of; and if we ask in faith, we will be given them. Jesus

Christ teaches, *"And all things, whatsoever ye shall ask in prayer, believing, ye shall receive."*[24] When we ask for those things that we know are right, then we can have faith that our Heavenly Father will grant our petitions.

I find that I do not always have the wisdom to know if what I am asking for is the best thing for me. Therefore, at the end of my prayers I often add the phrase I learned from the Savior when he was praying in the Garden of Gethsemane, *"nevertheless not what I will, but what thou wilt."*[25] Since Heavenly Father knows what is best for me, wants to help me to be successful, and can make more out of my life than I can, why shouldn't I yield to his judgment?

Once we have asked for help, then it is incumbent upon us to get up off our knees and do all that is within our power to help bring about the desired result of our prayers. We must be careful that we are not treating Heavenly Father as if he were a cosmic servant who is standing by to grant our every wish, with us taking no thought but to ask.

For example, if we are going to pray for Mrs. Harrison because she is an elderly lady who lives alone and is very lonely, it would be equally important for us to take a moment and call or visit her from time to time. It is not appropriate for us to lay our burdens upon the Lord without exercising any effort on our part.

Once we have completed our prayers, we should pause and give our Father in Heaven time to respond to our prayers, to share his love for us, and to answer us through the feelings that come into our hearts and the thoughts that come into our minds.

I find that sometimes I am guilty of talking to Heavenly Father like he was on the other end of the phone, and when I am finished talking I hang up the phone without even giving him a chance to respond.

Step Four: Close in the name of Jesus Christ

When we have finished, we should close in the name of Jesus Christ, who is our advocate with the Father. Jesus said, *"I am the way, the truth, and the life: no man cometh unto the Father, but by me."*[26]

He also says, *"Whatsoever ye shall ask the Father **in my name**, he will give it [to] you."*[27]

The final word we should use in our prayer is "Amen." It means "So be it," or "Truly." It closes our petition and affirms the sincerity of our supplication.

These steps may be helpful in organizing our thoughts and feelings as we pray. Remember, though, that asking Heavenly Father in faith, with a sincere heart, and in the name of Jesus Christ for what is right is more important than the exact words of our prayers.

56   Prayer

Chapter Four

Who Receives Answers to Their Prayers?

———•———

*T*he most often repeated direction we receive in the Bible is to pray. And since Heavenly Father has instructed us to pray, is it not reasonable to suppose that he will answer your prayers?

The Savior taught, *"And I say unto you, Ask, and it shall be given you; seek, and ye shall find; knock, and it shall be opened unto you. For every one that asketh receiveth; and he that seeketh findeth; and to him that knocketh it shall be opened."*[28]

In two verses of scripture we are told six times that if we ask we will receive an answer to our prayers. It is important to believe in Jesus Christ, but perhaps it is even more important to believe the words of the Savior when he tells us that our prayers will be heard and answered.

What if I Do Not Feel Close to God?

But, you may ask, "Will God really answer my prayers if I have not done everything in my life that I should have done?" I think if our Father in Heaven only answered the prayers of the perfect, no one would ever receive an answer to their prayers because we have all made many mistakes.

If you do not feel close to your Heavenly Father, you usually do not feel like praying. However, this is probably when you need to pray the most. If you have been depending on your own wit and wisdom to get you through the challenges of life, then the good news is that things could be so much better than they currently are. When you invite the power of God into your life, you are utilizing the greatest resource available to man.

It is important to remember that when you do not feel close to your Father in Heaven, it is not because he has moved away from you, but that you have moved away from him. If you have not been communicating with him frequently each and every day of your life, then you are forgoing many blessings that can help you in every aspect of your life.

You need to take the initiative to call home and communicate with your kind and loving Heavenly

Father who will welcome your prayers. It is the most important relationship you will ever have.

If you feel the least bit hesitant to pray because you worry that your petitions might not be welcome, then you may want to review the teachings of Jesus Christ. When the Savior was being condemned by the scribes and the Pharisees for eating with sinners, he responded, *"They that are whole have no need of the physician, but they that are sick: I came not to call the righteous, but the sinners to repentance."*[29]

Our Heavenly Father wants to be successful and happy and is most pleased when one of his sons or daughters comes to him, especially if it is after a long absence. Jesus Christ said, *"...I say unto you, there is joy in the presence of the angels of God over one sinner that repenteth."*[30]

Sometimes I Feel Like the Prodigal Son

The Savior's marvelous parable of the prodigal son further reinforces the concept that all are welcome to petition Heavenly Father. When the younger of two sons asked his father to give him his inheritance, his request was granted. Upon receiving his inheritance, the younger son left home and traveled to a far country where he squandered all of it in riotous living.

Once all was gone, he was forced to find work. He took a job feeding swine to try and keep from starving to death. In time, he reached the point that he was so downcast and hungry that he longed for the husks he was feeding the pigs. At this point, he decided to return home to his father, to confess his sins and ask to be able to work for him as a servant.

When the word went out that the younger son was returning home, it was interesting to see the father's reaction. The scriptures record,

*"But when he was yet a great way off, his father saw him, and had compassion, and **ran**, and fell on his neck, and kissed him.*

"And the son said unto him., Father, I have sinned against heaven, and in thy sight, and am no more worthy to be called thy son.

"But the father said to his servants, Bring forth the best robe, and put it on him; and put a ring on his hand, and shoes on his feet: And bring hither the fatted calf, and kill it; and let us eat, and be merry.

"For this my son was dead, and is alive again; he was lost, and is found."[31]

The forgiving and loving father in this parable represents Heavenly Father, and the prodigal son could represent any one of us at various times in our lives. It is truly remarkable how merciful our Father in Heaven is and how unconditional his love is toward we who are his children. Who could doubt that he is glad to hear from us any time we sincerely approach him in prayer?

Our Heavenly Father is Not Like Our Earthly Father

Sometimes we tend to judge our Heavenly Father by what we may see in our earthly father, which is not always as positive as we would like. Such was the case with a friend of mine named Charles, who was dramatically influenced by both his earthly father and his Heavenly Father.

Three days after Charles was born, his father walked out on the family. A few years later, his mother remarried and in time Charles became attached to his stepfather. They developed a closeness that came from spending many hours together talking and building a trusting relationship.

During Charles's sophomore year in high school, he made a wonderful discovery. Although he had not previously excelled in sports, he decided to try out for the water polo team. What followed was nothing short of remarkable, for within a few weeks after joining the team, he was one of the most outstanding players in the school, eclipsing the performance of the veterans that had played for years.

In fact, Charles was so good that even as a sophomore he was ranked the third best player in the country at his position. He received considerable attention and respect, and life seemed good. Many colleges were already looking at Charles, and it seemed certain he would receive an athletic scholarship to a most prestigious university upon graduation.

However, this season of joy and fulfillment was shattered one day when his mother announced the dreadful news that she was getting a divorce. Charles could not believe his ears! This terrible reality was intensified when his stepfather not only moved out of town but also completely severed his ties with his stepson and never so much as checked to see if Charles was still alive.

Charles was devastated by the thought that he had been abandoned by both his natural father and his stepfather. He became bitter and angry at the world. He developed a hostile attitude, dropped out of the mainstream, and turned to speed and cocaine. Soon he was addicted and started selling drugs to support his habit. By the time he was a junior in high school, his drug addiction led to failing grades, which disqualified him from participation in his one love, the water polo team.

His failing grades and disqualification added to his depression and despair. He felt he had nothing left to live for. He closed himself in his room, stopped eating, and tried to shut out the rest of the world. He had hit rock bottom and lost all hope. Finally he decided as a last resort to turn to his other father, his Father in Heaven, for help. He prayed,

"Dear God, if you are there, I know that you are greater than I am. If you will help me, I will repay you someday, I don't know how, but I will."

After he finished praying, he stayed in his room for the rest of the week, away from the temptations and bad influences of the world. During this period, a remarkable metamorphosis began. Charles decided if Heavenly Father was going to help him, then he would stop using cocaine and speed and would change his life. From that day on, never once did Charles ever return to the drugs that had previously consumed his life.

Although he knew he could not turn his life around by himself, he found that with Heavenly Father's help, the one father that would not let him down, he could not only overcome his depression, but he could create a new life that would be worth living.

When Charles did turn to Heavenly Father for help, he found love, compassion, forgiveness, mercy, and the strength to do what he could not do alone. He began to attend church and to try to improve his life.

Although it has been more than twenty years since Charles petitioned his Heavenly Father for help to escape from his valley of despair, never has his love and devotion for God wavered. Today he is a successful businessman, has a wonderful family, and volunteers at his church. He continues to seek ways to try and repay his Father for blessing his life so richly.

Heavenly Father is happy when the prodigal returns and asks for help in turning his life around. And it is important to realize that Father in Heaven did not wait until Charles had stopped using drugs and was living an exemplary life before he would listen to his prayers and help him. If that were a prerequisite, Charles would never have had the strength to overcome his addiction.

I believe that our Father's love for us is unconditional. He loves us in spite of our failings and weaknesses, and if we will turn to him, he can help us climb the mountain we cannot climb alone.

Opening the Windows of Heaven

Even if Heavenly Father is willing to help the prodigal, he is much happier if we will live his commandments and follow in the footsteps of the Savior, Jesus Christ. When we are living the kind of life that we know is approved by God, it is much easier to pray with the faith needed to receive answers to our prayers and bring the blessings of heaven into our lives.

Heavenly Father will be able to help us develop the characteristics of a just and righteous person much more quickly if we are continuously communicating with him. It will also allow our Father in Heaven to open doors for us that would otherwise be closed if we were not living a virtuous life.

I have a good friend named Lenore who is committed to living a good life and serving other people. Heavenly Father is mindful of the integrity of her heart and her love for him. Because of the love she had for her Father in Heaven, it was easy for her to turn to him in a moment of desperation when her life hung in the balance. This is her story:

"A couple of weeks after undergoing major surgery, I began to experience a shortness of breath. My anxiety grew as my breathing became more labored, so I called my doctor. He prescribed something to curb my anxiety and help me sleep. He told me to call him in the morning if I felt the same. The next morning I still didn't feel well, but I sent my children off to school and my husband to work.

"The shortness of breath continued, but I was reluctant to call my doctor in case it really was just anxiety. I became so frightened and weakened that I felt I couldn't even make a responsible decision.

"In desperation I cried out in prayer, pleading to my Father in Heaven for help. I told him that I did not know what was best for me and that I needed his help. Shortly thereafter, my doctor called saying he wanted me at the nearby hospital within 30 minutes for a lung scan.

I rushed to get dressed and to find a ride to the hospital. With no time to spare, I hurriedly checked in at the front desk and then ran down the corridors to the appointed area.

"After the scan began, the technician left the room. Then, suddenly, I stopped breathing. Just as I began to feel that my life was over, I felt a strong reassurance that I would be alright, and slowly I began to breathe again. When the technician returned, she insisted I remain prone and try not to move.

A couple of minutes later she handed me a phone. My doctor was on the other end. He informed me I had 3 pulmonary embolisms and I would be admitted immediately to the hospital. Instantly, I recalled the possible complications of surgery and realized that even one blood clot in the lungs can be fatal. For the next week-and-a-half, I lingered between life and death. But gradually I regained my strength and was eventually discharged from the hospital.

"Once I had been home for awhile, I had occasion to talk to my doctor again and learned how my Heavenly Father had intervened to save my life. The doctor told me that upon arriving at his office the morning after our conversation he felt an urgent need to order a lung scan for me. Immediately he began calling one facility after another to schedule an appointment, but no one had an available slot.

When he was about to give up, a representative from the closest hospital called him back saying they would fit me in if I arrived within half an hour. This process took place while I was pouring my heart out in prayer and asking my Father in Heaven for help. Although I didn't know what I needed, a loving

Heavenly Father was opening doors for me that would save my life."

I believe that Heavenly Father hears the prayers of the righteous and loves to bless their lives.

God answers the prayers of the prodigal, the righteous, and everyone in between, regardless of their position or title. In the book of Acts in the New Testament, Peter teaches us that *"God is no respecter of persons."*[32]

Our Father in Heaven does not give greater attention to the king, prime minister, or president than he does to the laborer, janitor, or maid. They are all his children and have the same right to call upon him.

I have had thousands of prayers answered in my life, and they have improved the quality of my life immeasurably. I have had my life saved on several occasions and have been lifted out of caverns of despair because a gracious, loving, and forgiving God has answered my prayers.

Chapter Five

How Does Our Heavenly Father Answer Prayers?

———••———

*W*hen we pray it seems that most of our energy is devoted to asking, pleading, requesting, explaining, justifying, apologizing, or in other words, talking. But after we have spoken, how much time do we set aside for listening, hearing, receiving, or understanding what our Heavenly Father's will is regarding our petitions?

How does our Father in Heaven answer our prayers? Is it normal to receive visions, dreams, or visitations, or to hear voices speaking to us in answer to our prayers? If we study the Bible, we may think this is a perfectly normal, everyday occurrence and wonder why we are not receiving the same. I think that on occasion, our Father in Heaven may choose to use any one of these methods to communicate with us, but usually he does not. It is well to remember that these more dramatic forms of revelation recorded in the Bible were of such a magnitude that they were given a special place in those sacred records, providing guidance and hope for countless millions of people over many centuries.

So you may ask, "How will my prayers be answered?"

Heavenly Father speaks to us through the "*still small voice.*"[33] This still, small voice is the Holy Spirit as it speaks to our mind and heart. After we have finished praying, if we will be still and receptive, our Father in Heaven may answer our prayers through a stream of thoughts that flows into our minds, or impressions that we feel in our heart. These feelings are positive, calming, and warming, and they reassure us that all is well and that Heavenly Father has heard us and loves us. We must be quiet and receptive if we are to receive and understand God's will for us.

Sometimes we may receive these thoughts or feelings immediately after we pray, and sometimes they may come hours or even days later while we are thinking about the issue, or while we are relaxed and quiet. The Psalmist counsels us to *"Be still and know that [he is] God."*[34]

If we are still and quiet, our Father in Heaven will use the Holy Spirit not only to answer our prayers but also to bring things to our remembrance, to teach, to comfort, and to warn us.

Listening for the Still, Small Voice

It is easy to get caught up in the hustle and bustle of our busy world and lose awareness that the still, small voice even exists. I am reminded of a situation that recently took place in my life that taught me an important lesson.

While I was driving to an appointment, I made an important phone call to a person I needed to talk to before the meeting started. But there was no answer, just voicemail. I left a message and then stayed off the phone in hopes of receiving a return call before my appointment.

It took another twenty minutes to reach my destination, and I was listening to the radio as I drove. It was disappointing to not receive the return call prior to arriving at the meeting place.

After the meeting was over, I returned to my car and started for home. Listening to my voicemail messages I discovered that I had received the much anticipated return call. To my sorrow, I found that the critical call came in while I was driving to my appointment, but since the ringer on the phone was set on the "soft" ring, I did not hear it over the sound of the radio.

This experience caused me to wonder how often my Heavenly Father tries to speak to me by the "still, small voice" to answer my prayers or to give me inspiration or guidance, but I am too busy or otherwise preoccupied to hear him.

The Still, Small Voice Comes to Those with Faith

There are some people who live their lives with absolute faith in Heavenly Father and follow the promptings of the still, small voice. He is therefore able to do some wonderful things through them. Such was the case with a young mother named Alice.

It was a typical January day in Cedar City: gray and overcast, with snow falling. Alice had taken her husband to work, sent the children off to school, run a number of errands, returned home, cleaned the house, and started dinner. It was now two o'clock in the afternoon, and she realized that she had an entire hour to herself.

This was a rare and wonderful opportunity. She decided that she would spend this precious time reading and relaxing. But almost as soon as she sat down, the strongest feeling came to her that she needed to go and pick up her husband from work. She thought, "This is silly, there is plenty of time before I have to leave." So she went back to her reading. Again that still, small voice within her said, "Look outside. You'd better go now." She glanced outside and was surprised to see that conditions had changed dramatically, and it looked like the snow storm might soon become a blizzard. She quietly said to herself, "Yes, I'd better go now."

Alice hurriedly wrote a note to her children telling them that she had gone to pick up Dad. Then she left the house. As she neared the town, she could see through the snow the faint shadow of a man leaving a gas station and walking along the side of the road. As Alice got closer to him, the still, small voice within her again prompted her, "Help this man, he is your neighbor." She thought, "I do not know him. He is a stranger. I am a woman alone in a blizzard, and I am afraid." She was not going to stop, but again the still, small voice within her said, "Help him!"

She gently pulled the car to the side of the road and rolled the window down a few inches and nervously asked, "May I help you?" Suddenly the back door of the car flew open and a large truck tire was placed in her old station wagon. Then the passenger side door opened and a wind-blown, half-frozen young man climbed into the car.

He expressed his heartfelt appreciation that she had stopped. She asked, "Where do you need to go?" He directed her down an old country highway away from town. She turned the car around and as they started to drive away, the young man's emotions erupted as he began to unfold the precarious events of the day.

He explained that he was a farmer, and seeing the brewing storm blowing in, decided to drive into town to the feed store. He took the spare tire out of his old truck so there would be room for as much feed as possible. He placed his three-year-old son on the seat beside him and started off. About half way to town his front tire blew out. He had no spare. He was in terrible trouble! It was getting very cold as the wind and snow increased in intensity. He was miles from town and there was no one to help him.

What should he do? Should he take his little son out of the truck and try to make it to town, or should he take the tire off and leave his little boy by himself in the truck and carry the tire into town? He hated the thought of taking his precious little son out in the hostile weather. But he was afraid to leave him alone. What if the little one got out of the truck and wandered off, or someone took him, or another car crashed into his stranded truck because of the whiteout conditions?

There were no good choices, and he did not know what to do. He bowed his head and pleaded with all his heart for his Father in Heaven to help him. He jacked up the truck, took the tire off, and put out flares around the disabled truck. Then he bundled up his little boy the best he could and told him to stay in the truck until Daddy got back. He thought his heart would break as he said goodbye to his little son, who had tears streaming down his face and which were mirrored by those that filled his own eyes.

Every step he took towards town, away from his son, increased the anxiety in his heart. By now he was pleading with his Heavenly Father to watch over his son. He also begged the Lord to help him get his tire fixed as quickly as possible.

Alice listened intently as her young passenger poured out his heart as they traveled toward the abandoned truck that contained the precious cargo. Suddenly he shouted, "There it is!" She could just make out the outline of the truck which was now coated with snow. She pulled over, he thanked her profusely and grabbed the tire out of her back seat and ran towards his stranded vehicle.

Once she saw that the little boy was safe and the tire was remounted, she drove back to town to pick up her husband. During those quiet moments of reflection, Alice realized that she had been enlisted by her Heavenly Father to help him answer this young father's earnest prayers. A wave of warmth and peace swept into her heart. My, how happy she was that she had the faith to obey the promptings of the still, small voice. Sometimes Heavenly Father answers our prayers when the still, small voice speaks to another whom God has enlisted to assist us.

Living Worthy to Receive Revelation from God

The Spirit of God will not dwell in us or inspire us if we are not keeping the commandments of God. We must become the kind of person that the Spirit will not be offended to be around. Once we have trained ourselves to live righteously and to listen to the promptings of the Spirit, we will recognize answers to our prayers more readily. This training will also allow Heavenly Father to greatly benefit our lives.

Promptings or inspiration can come suddenly, especially when needed to help others. Such was the case a couple of years ago, while I was sitting in a meeting with Phil, a friend of mine. After a few minutes, Phil quietly stated, "I need to call my father." He excused himself from the meeting and made the phone call. When he returned, he shared with us that his father was in very poor health, struggling to breathe, and was yearning for contact from him. Phil also told us that his father, with few words, expressed his great appreciation for the call and reinforced the bond of love between them when he said, "I knew you would call."

Our Heavenly Father attended to the needs of this faithful father by inspiring his son, who was 800 miles away, to interrupt what he was doing to make this important call.

Father in Heaven is a kind and loving parent who knows our needs even before we ask. If we are living a worthy life sometimes he will warn us of danger even before we pray. One such experience occurred in the life of Cynthia. She recounts,

"I was working at my job as a medical technologist in a reference laboratory. The thought popped into mind, "What will you do when the earthquake comes?" Just as quickly I thought, "Where did that come from?" Again the prompting came into my mind, "What will you do when the earthquake comes?" I began looking around the laboratory and bench area for a safe place where I would be sheltered from moving instruments or flying glass.

"The lab benches were anchored from the floor to the ceiling with steel poles, and underneath the bench tops, boxes of supplies were stored. I found a section next to an anchored pole and once I removed a large empty box, there was plenty of room for a person to crouch and hold onto the pole. I was satisfied I had, for whatever reason, acted on that thought.

"A short time later, at 5:05 p.m., I was working at my computer when the Loma Prieta Earthquake struck. Right next to where I was sitting was a large heavy bookshelf filled with books, papers, and some boxed supplies. By the time I realized what was happening, the things on the shelf began to fall toward me. I immediately darted toward the laboratory bench I had prepared, ducked under it, and securely held onto a pole. It was then that I realized, had I not been prepared beforehand, I would have been injured.

"I have not always obeyed the promptings of the still small voice in my life, but this experience taught me that I must live to be worthy to receive this communication from God at all times and to always be responsive to it."

Sometimes we receive revelation that saves us from harm, and sometimes we receive it so that we can protect the life of another. I know a mother named Jenny who tells the following remarkable story of how she was inspired to save the life of her daughter.

"Shortly after Megan, our second daughter, was born, she wouldn't settle down and go to sleep unless we were holding her. It was the middle of the night, and I was exhausted, so my husband Brent offered to hold her. I think I fell asleep before my head even hit the pillow. Suddenly I awoke and sat up. I was impressed by the Spirit to go and check on Megan. I felt as if I had been asleep for hours, but I looked at the clock and I had only been asleep for 15 minutes. I fell back in the bed and thought, 'I don't need to check her already.'

"Again the still, small voice prompted me to go and check on Megan. I went into the living room and found both my husband and daughter were asleep. Her little head had slipped down between our beanbag chair and Brent's arm so that she couldn't breathe. I quickly took her into my arms and thanked my Father in Heaven for the prompting that helped me save her from danger."

Receiving Inspiration to Guide Our Lives

When we are continuously in communication with our Father in Heaven, it is much easier to recognize and receive the revelation and inspiration he sends to guide us in making the decisions that will help us in overcoming the challenges of life.

Some years ago, when my wife and I were driving to visit my wife's parents, we ran into a terrible, blinding snowstorm. We were in a desolate area where we did not want to stop, but the snow was coming down so heavily that it was very difficult to keep the car on the road. We prayed for safety and help as we continued our journey.

Then a large trailer truck passed us that did not seem to have as much trouble navigating through the storm. We decided to catch up with the truck and stay right behind it. We found that if we stopped focusing on the snow storm and just kept our eyes on the lights of the truck in front of us, we had no problem continuing our journey behind our newly adopted guide. We successfully continued our journey in this manner for several hundred miles and arrived safely at our destination.

I think if we train ourselves to be sensitive and receptive to the promptings of the Holy Spirit as our Heavenly Father communicates to us through the still, small voice, it will serve as our guide through any challenge we may have in life. Once we become acquainted with these warm and peaceful feelings of affirmation, love, and peace, we will never want to be without them. These feelings help reinforce our confidence in Heavenly Father's love for us and his willingness to answer our prayers and come to our aid.

A wonderful lady by the name of Cheryl tells of feeling the promptings from the still, small voice, which helped her find her way when she did not know where to go.

She said, "I had a business meeting which took me out of town. After I had been driving for a long time, I discovered that I had forgotten my planner, which contained the address of the place where my meeting was to be held.

"There was no way I could return home and still make my meeting on time. I wondered what I should do. I felt impressed to pray. I pulled the car over, prayed, and asked Heavenly Father to show me the way to go. As I began driving, I felt I should take a certain exit off the freeway, then felt prompted to turn first at one corner, then another and then another.

"As I looked up the street after making the third turn, I saw some people walking up to a house that turned out to be the destination of my meeting. My Heavenly Father had answered my prayers through the guidance of the Spirit speaking to my mind and heart."

Blessings Come According to God's Time Frame

It is important to realize that spiritual experiences like receiving the promptings of the Spirit cannot be forced; they must be done in God's time frame and in his way. We must be careful not to become impatient or annoyed because we are not receiving answers as quickly as we would like. I know it is difficult to wait patiently for answers that we would like to receive now! On occasion, I have joked that I have lots of patience because I have never used any of it.

Someone wrote:
> With thoughtless and impatient hands
> We tangle up the plans
> The Lord hath wrought,
> And when we cry in pain, He saith,
> "Be quiet, man, while I untie the knot."

Some Answers to Prayer Come Only After Study

On occasion, Heavenly Father may want us to wait to receive an answer, or he may give it to us in degrees as we are prepared to receive it. And sometimes he may want us to do more than just ask him for help. He may want us to think, ponder, and study the issues that we have prayed to have resolved. At these times, we must examine our options and then, based on our analysis, select what we think and feel is the best option. Once we have done this, then we can take the matter to our Heavenly Father and ask him if what we have chosen really is the best option for us to pursue.

During and after we have prayed, we should be sensitive to the thoughts that come into our mind and the feelings that come into our heart. If the feelings are positive, make us feel good, and fill us with warmth, peace, and joy, then they are of the Spirit and it is a verification that what we have proposed to our Father is right for us. If we have no such feeling, then we might continue to question the option we have selected.

The process of pondering, or meditating, means to think deeply about or contemplate the subject. This process allows us to do our part in working with the Spirit so that Heavenly Father is not just handing us the answer without any effort on our part.

A friend of mine named Steve had an experience where he was required to do more than just ask before his prayer was answered. He tells of the time when he lost a ring of keys that were very important to him, as he needed them to get into his office. It was a weekend, and he looked everywhere he could think of during the next two days, but he could not find them. His family looked—they pulled up cushions, looked in the car and in pockets, and retraced steps—but they could not find the keys.

The night before he was to go to work, he decided to go to his Heavenly Father in prayer. He knelt beside his desk and offered the following prayer:

"Heavenly Father, I know you have more important things to worry about than this, but I have lost my keys, and I have looked everywhere I can think to look, but I cannot find them. I need them to get into my office. Please help me to find them."

After he finished talking to God in prayer, he sat down and began to ponder the situation. After he had been thinking about it for a time, a vision came into his mind and he could see where the keys were located. He found they had fallen through the hole in his desk that allowed the electrical cords to run down behind the desk to the wall.

The keys had fallen to the floor and were hidden behind a strong box and some other items that were located under the desk. It was clear that he would not have found the keys in time without the assistance of heaven. It is important to note that it was while he was sitting quietly, pondering about the situation, that Heavenly Father inspired him to see in his mind the location of the missing keys.

A young woman named Joyce learned the power of pondering when she had a problem she had to solve. She remembers,

"I was recently married and working at a women's clothing store. At the end of the day, the cash in the register didn't match the sales. Since I was the only one working the cash register, it looked like I stole the money. I racked my brain trying to figure out where I had made the mistake, but no answers came to mind.

"I had to leave work not knowing what I had done wrong. When I got home, I went on a walk to think and ponder about the situation and to try and clear my mind. I kept going over the day in my mind. I did that over and over. As I pondered the situation, I prayed about it and asked Heavenly Father to help me. I had done all that I knew how to do on my own, and now I needed to take the problem to the Lord. I knew He knew what I had done wrong.

"As I prayed with fervency, I felt a warm, tingly feeling all over my body witnessing to me that I was about to receive an answer. There in front of me was a mental picture of the two items that a lady had put on lay-away earlier that day. I could even see the price typed in below the items. I had rung it up as a cash sale instead of a lay-away.

"I ran home and called my manager, thanking my Heavenly Father all the way for the answer He so kindly gave me."

Tuning Out the Interference

Some people have found that it is difficult to be still and to quietly ponder about the challenges of life. In fact, in our busy, fast-paced world, we come to think of being quiet as wasting time. We may even find we are uncomfortable if we are not doing something all the time. If we are driving somewhere we must be listening to the radio or talking on the phone; otherwise we think we are not making good use of our time. We would be wise to train ourselves to think, pray, and ponder while we are alone. Sometimes we should keep the radio off and forget about the things of the world. We should learn to focus more on the things that really matter the most, the things of eternity.

We need to train ourselves to tune out the interference caused by the noise and turmoil of the world. I am reminded of a situation that takes place each time we get on board a commercial airliner. Before the plane can take off, the flight attendants ask you to turn off all electronic equipment and to keep your cell phone off during the entire flight. This is important because they do not want any interference between the pilot and the air traffic controllers. It certainly would be disconcerting if the pilot had to try and figure out which of many concurrent voices he was hearing was the actual air traffic controller.

If we prepare ourselves by being peaceful and quiet, we will be more sensitive to the Spirit and will have an easier time communicating with our Father in Heaven. As an ancient Chinese proverb states, "When the student is ready the teacher will appear."

Beware of Promptings from the Wrong Source

It is so important to train ourselves to be receptive to revelation, inspiration, or the promptings from the Spirit as it will greatly enrich our lives. At the same time, it is noteworthy that all revelation does not come from Heavenly Father and the Holy Spirit. We can also receive promptings or thoughts from the adversary of all men, Satan, or the Devil as he is referred to in the Bible. But as Paul counsels, *"Neither give place to the devil."*[35]

"But put on the whole armour of God, that ye may be able to stand against the wiles of the devil."[36]

James directs, *"Submit yourselves therefore to God. Resist the devil, and he will flee from you. Draw nigh to God, and he will draw nigh to you."*[37]

Promptings from the Devil never try to persuade us to do anything right or ever to turn to God. They are negative, they do not make us feel good, and they will never help us to progress or to find happiness. We cannot do wrong and feel right about it.

On the other hand, we need to be able to recognize the "fruit" of the Spirit of God as it was identified by the apostle Paul when he said, *"...the fruit of the Spirit is love, joy, peace, longsuffering, gentleness, goodness, faith, meekness, temperance...."*[38] James adds, *"The wisdom that is from above is first pure, then peaceable, gentle, and easy to be intreated, full of mercy and good fruits, without partiality, and without hypocrisy. And the fruit of righteousness is sown in peace of them that make peace."*[39]

If we want to cultivate a place in our hearts for these positive feelings, we must stay out of Satan's territory by avoiding inappropriate movies, videos, television programs, video games, and music, and by shunning pornography of any kind. Keep your thoughts clean and pure and do not let the Devil introduce lustful thoughts into your mind. As someone has said, "We may not be able to keep a bird from landing on our heads, but we do not have to let him build a nest there." Do not harbor ill feelings, hatred, or envy in your heart.

As soon as an inappropriate thought comes into your mind, immediately substitute a virtuous thought for it. Think about a favorite passage of scripture that you have memorized, or think of the words of a hymn you like. Remember, you are a child of God and he knows of all you do. Be a righteous representative of your Father in Heaven and of your Savior, Jesus Christ.

There is so much the Father offers his children if they will do as he asks. We do not want to forfeit this wonderful inheritance by being lured away by the Devil. We should follow the example that Jesus Christ set for us. When Satan came trying to tempt him after he had been fasting for forty days, Jesus continued to resist his temptations until the Devil departed from him.

I have had a great many prayers answered in my life. Some of my petitions were answered immediately, even before I finished praying, others not answered for some time after I asked and others were answered in ways I had not expected. Some of my prayers dealt with matters of life and death, but most of them pertained to the small and simple things of life. Besides offering morning and evening prayers, I offer a continual stream of requests and communications to my Father in Heaven every day.

I know with absolute certainty that God answers prayers. I have also come to know that when my petitions are not granted, it is what is best for me. The one thing that has been consistent in all of my communications with my Heavenly Father is that I feel his great love, forgiveness, and kindness towards me and all of his children.

Chapter Six

When the Windows of Heaven Seem Closed

———••———

*W*hen we consider the number of times that the scriptures promise us answers to our prayers, why is it that sometimes we cannot get an answer, regardless of how earnestly we ask?

Since Heavenly Father has the power to grant our requests, should we assume he is not happy with us, has lost interest in us, or just doesn't care what we want?

If none of these reasons are valid, then why do our petitions occasionally seem to fall upon deaf ears when it seems other people have no trouble receiving answers to their prayers? Perhaps it would be helpful to explore some of the reasons why we may not be receiving the answer we have petitioned our Father in Heaven to send us.

Why Does Heavenly Father Say No?

Because the Lord knows that in some situations what we are asking for is not what is best for us, the answer to some prayers will be "No." We should remember that he knows everything and we know very little. We may accept this fact, or we may respond in the same way that we did when we were little children and our earthly parents said "No." We may become upset with our Heavenly Parent and figuratively stamp our feet. But it will do no good; the answer will still be "No."

When Tanner was three years old, he invited a little friend over to the house for a play date. Tanner and his friend played well together for several hours. When it was time for his friend to leave, his mother stuck her head into his room only to discover that the room was completely trashed to the point that every single toy and game was dumped on the floor and even the sheets were taken from the bed.

Once his friend left, his mother told Tanner that he would have to clean up his room as soon as he got back from preschool. Before he left the house, Mother saw Tanner kneeling in prayer. After he had finished praying, she asked him if he was praying that his room would be clean by the time he returned home. He admitted that this was what he was praying about. Mom told him that Heavenly Father does not always answer "Yes" to all prayers because sometimes an affirmative answer would not be what is best for us. When Tanner returned from preschool and entered his room, he was sad to see that the mess was indeed still there.

We may try to persuade our Father to change his mind by pleading, but it is well to remember that not only does he understand our needs better than we do, he also knows the future.

We may make an earnest plea such as, "Heavenly Father, please do not let my child die, I will do anything you ask if you will make her well. Our little daughter is so sweet, beautiful, and innocent, we love her so much, please do not take her from us." It seems so logical to us that God would say "Yes" when what we are asking for is good, kind, and compassionate. How could Heavenly Father say "No" to our earnest pleadings?

In fact, this is the very situation that faced a young father some years ago. What follows are the fervent, tender feelings of a sensitive father named Michael as his family struggled and prayed to save the life of their daughter.

"I breathed a sigh of relief when I heard the baby's cry come from the emergency room of the hospital where I had just rushed my wife, Shanna, and our infant daughter, Lindsay. Shanna had just delivered Lindsay, our baby daughter. I thought everything was going to be okay until I learned that Lindsay's lung had collapsed and that she had had no oxygen for almost 10 minutes. The news struck me like a rock, and I realized that we would now have to pray for a miracle—that Lindsay would live and would have a healthy brain and body.

"When the doctor did not give us much encouragement, I took the problem to Heavenly Father. I have never prayed so long or so hard in my life. I have never cried so much in my life. I have never expressed so much faith in my life. I can't imagine any torture or trial that could be worse than losing your child. It has to be the *extreme* test of faith. However, my faith never wavered, even as I prayed to Heavenly Father to take my house, cars, savings accounts, and even the clothes off my back if he would just save her.

"While walking in front of the hospital and in the waiting room late that evening, I felt strangely at peace, as though everything would be okay, no matter what the odds. But what was I really feeling? Was Heavenly Father saying, 'She will be made well, but not upon this earth, for I need her in heaven'?

"Oh, how often we take life for granted, and I almost took Lindsay's life for granted until that day when her small lung collapsed. For a short period of time, I felt so good about the situation, and it looked like she was improving. My prayers began to lessen in intensity.

"I went alone to the hospital before work Monday morning to spend a few precious moments with Lindsay. I was back at lunchtime, admiring her strength and feeling encouraged by her good color, never imagining that within half an hour after returning to work, I would receive a phone call from my sweet wife asking me to meet her at the chaplain's office in the hospital. Not until that point had I allowed myself to feel that death was actually a possibility. When the doctor told us she was gone, I tried to be strong; but inside, how I cried!

"Our beautiful daughter left us after three days of fighting to stay on this earth. I know in my heart it was God's will. It had to be, for many hundreds of people were praying for a miracle. But knowing where Lindsay is does not take away the feelings of pain and loss.

"I have faith that our Lindsay is now with our Father in Heaven, and I know we will again meet her someday. I don't know why this had to happen, but rather than asking 'Why me?' I have chosen to use this experience to help me appreciate every life and every moment of life and to know that God had to have an extremely important reason to take her from our arms."

The great prophet Isaiah teaches us a truth that may help us to understand why our kind and loving Father in Heaven may not answer our prayers in a way that we are convinced makes perfect sense. Isaiah directs us to call upon our Father in Heaven, and then he adds a reminder that we do not think or act the way God does. He says, *"For my thoughts are not your thoughts, neither are your ways my ways, saith the Lord. For as the heavens are higher than the earth, so are my ways higher than your ways, and my thoughts than your thoughts."*[40]

We must remember we are not at the same level as our Father in Heaven. We will never think of something that did not already occur to him or propose a solution that he has not thought of until we brought it to his attention. He is a perfect and all-knowing God. He gets it right the first time and every time. We need to humble ourselves and recognize this whenever we address him.

Even if we compare a wise, intelligent, just, and compassionate earthly father having a conversation with his two-year-old toddler, to our relationship with God, it would still not adequately demonstrate the distance in thinking and knowledge between us and our omnipotent, perfect Heavenly Father.

In the same way that our experienced earthly parents understood that what we wanted as children may not have been what was best for us, our wise, compassionate, and perfect Father in Heaven knows exactly what is best for his children and may bless us by not allowing us to have what we ask for.

Perhaps when our sojourn in mortality is over, we will better understand why we did not get everything that we asked for. In the meantime, we should follow the pattern that our Savior, Jesus Christ, demonstrated when in the Garden of Gethsemane. He pleaded with his Father to take the bitter cup from him but then ended his prayer with the phrase, *"Nevertheless not my will, but thine, be done."*[41] In spite of what Jesus asked for, he wanted most of all to do his Father's will. This concept was also taught by the Savior when he gave us the Lord's Prayer: *"Thy will be done...."*[42]

Have We Really Understood?

Sadly, sometimes we do receive an affirmative answer to our prayers, but we fail to notice it or we do not understand it. The answer may come through the actions of another, through inspiration coming into our mind that we mistakenly attribute to our own wisdom, or through the still, small voice of the Spirit that we cannot hear because we are not listening.

I remember one night when our seven-year-old daughter, Hailey, got out of bed and came in to see her mother and me. She was crying as she said in a mild panic, "There is something in my throat and I can't swallow." I took her into the kitchen to give her some juice. As I was pouring the juice, she confided, "I prayed to Heavenly Father and He did not help me."

I was impressed that she had independently sought help through prayer and was not surprised when she expected to instantly receive an answer to her petition. I gave her some juice and told her, "Heavenly Father did hear your prayer and that is why I am giving you juice right now." She thought about it for a few minutes, and after she drank down the juice, she smiled and said, "Thank you Heavenly Father."

How often are we guilty of dashing off a prayer and not even taking the time to listen for an answer? We may never pause long enough to understand the answer that a willing Heavenly Father has given us.

Will We Wait for an Answer to Our Prayers?

Sometimes what we have prayed for is okay with our Father in Heaven, but he has determined that what is best for us is to wait for a time before he grants our request. However, if we become impatient and irritable because our petition is not immediately granted, we may falsely suppose that God has not answered our prayers or that the heavens are closed to us.

A lady named Lenore tells the story about what happened to her daughter and son-in-law that taught them that waiting until Heavenly Father was ready to grant their petitions greatly improved the outcome of what they received.

Their courtship and wedding seemed like a fairy tale come true. Both Mark and Colleen were hard-working, bright, and looking forward to a promising future. Mark was hoping to be accepted into law school as he had applied for admission to several universities.

Then he received his first rejection letter. "Oh well," they reassured themselves, "there were other law schools." They felt confident that he would be entering one in the fall. Some time later, after receiving their last rejection letter, they realized that new plans would have to be made. It seemed very unfair! They struggled to understand why God would allow this to happen to them when they had both worked so hard and were so constant in their prayers.

Mark got a job so that Colleen could stay home with their new baby daughter. During the next year Mark had some health problems, but they were nothing his doctor thought to be serious.

During the following year Mark reapplied for admission to several law schools. Again there were rejection letters, but this time they also received an acceptance letter. So Mark quit his job, and they moved to a new area of the country.

One week after Mark's classes started, he became seriously ill and was rushed to the hospital. The physician on duty immediately diagnosed Mark as having a chronic condition known as Crohn's Disease.

The doctor, a leading gastroenterologist, was known as one of the best for his expertise in diagnosing and treating patients with Crohn's Disease. During Mark's first year of school, he was hospitalized three times and underwent major surgery. The medical expenses could have been devastating if not for the medical insurance he had acquired while he was working. The physician, understanding the financial stress Mark was under, offered to write off the medical expenses not covered by the insurance.

What Mark and Colleen didn't know when they were first praying for Mark to be admitted into law school was that he had a very serious condition that would require the right doctor and the resources to treat it. But God knew it.

If Mark had been accepted into law school the first year, he would not have had the benefit of being introduced to one of the best doctors for treating his illness. He would not have had the insurance coverage to pay for the very expensive medical treatments. Once you've been diagnosed with a serious chronic illness like Crohn's Disease, no insurance company wants to insure you. Fortunately, the insurance plan offered to him while he was working continued to cover his additional surgeries, hospitalizations, tests, and expensive drug treatments over the years.

Sometimes our finite minds don't always know what is best for us at the time, but God has infinite wisdom and can use it to bless our lives in ways that benefit us the most.

Are We Praying Directly to Heavenly Father?

Perhaps one reason our petitions are not answered is that we fail to follow the teachings of the Savior, who taught us to pray directly to our Heavenly Father. If we are not praying directly to our Father in Heaven, we are not doing what the Savior taught us to do in the Lord's prayer. Jesus Christ said, *"After this manner therefore pray ye: Our Father which art in heaven, Hallowed be thy name."*[43]

If we are not praying to our Heavenly Father, why would we expect him to answer us? After all, we don't answer someone who is not talking to us.

The fact that I do not have to go through any appointment secretaries or assistants, nor do I have to make an appointment to talk with our loving Heavenly Father, reinforces in my mind that I am a beloved child of God. It also helps me to stay focused, be humble, and to treat my Father in Heaven with reverence, respect, and love.

Are We Praying with Faith?

The apostle Paul tells us, *"But **without faith** it is impossible to please him: for he that cometh to God must believe that he is, and that he is a rewarder of them that diligently seek him."*[44] Jesus Christ instructed us to believe and we would receive: *"Therefore I say unto you, What things soever ye desire, when ye pray, **believe that ye receive them**, and ye shall have them."*[45]

A faithful young mother was having trouble with her children, and in faith she turned to God for help. She said, "Our two little sons fought like wild cats. I couldn't understand it. It concerned me terribly. Everyone I talked to offered a different solution. None worked. Finally, I decided to make it a matter of prayer. The night I engaged in prayer, I had faith I would be given an answer. I felt compelled to have the house completely orderly; the washing and ironing done, everything tidy, clean, etc.

"A few minutes before midnight, I bathed and began my prayer. I asked God why one of my sons behaved the way he did. The divine instruction I received left me spiritually breathless. It was a vivid and very personal answer, which humbles me to this day—gentle, rebuking, and very instructive."

When we have been living the commandments and doing what we know Heavenly Father wants us to do, we have greater confidence and faith in being able to ask and receive an answer to our prayers. As Henry Ward Beecher once said, "*It is not well for a man to pray cream and live skim milk.*"

The apostle James reminds us of the importance of praying with faith: "*But let him **ask in faith**, nothing wavering. For he that wavereth is like a wave of the sea driven with the wind and tossed.*"[46]

A friend named Dan made this insightful comment: "Sometimes we lack faith in ourselves to be able to receive an answer to our prayers. Even though we might believe that Heavenly Father can do anything, we don't think he will do it for us. We lack confidence in our ability to receive the answer." However, we need to believe Jesus Christ when he tells us that Heavenly Father will answer *our* prayers when we ask in faith.

Are We Asking God to Do Everything?

Sometimes when an answer doesn't come, it is because we have done nothing except ask. We have not taken time to study it out, weigh the various options, select the best choice, and then ask if it is right. We want Heavenly Father to do it all.

Perhaps some of us fall into the habit of treating God as if he were our own personal cosmic servant who, like a genie, is just standing by, waiting to fulfill our every desire. If this is true, then we are likely to be very disappointed in the results of our prayers.

Someone once said, "You should pray as if everything depended upon God and then get up off your knees and work as if everything depended upon you." This practice was well demonstrated in an experience that Stan, a friend of mine, shared with me.

One day, while Stan was living in Minnesota, the temperature dropped to about 40 degrees below zero. He had some important business he needed to take care of, and when he went to start his car, nothing happened. He spent an hour trying to defrost the engine with the assistance of a hair dryer, but it would not even turn over.

After he had done all he could think to do, Stan went into the house and prayed and asked Heavenly Father to help. Then he went back out and tried again, and the car started up just like it was a summer day. Heavenly Father only expects us to do what we can do. Then he will do the rest.

Are Our Prayers Sincere?

If we do not pray with sincerity and real intent, we are not offering an acceptable prayer to our Father in Heaven. Prayers are as much feelings as they are words. We need to pray honestly and put our hearts and minds into what we are saying. We need to stay focused on whom we are talking to and what we are saying and not let our minds wander.

In Shakespeare's *Hamlet*, Claudius stopped praying because his prayers stopped being meaningful. He said, *"My words fly up, my thoughts remain below: Words without thoughts never to heaven go."*[47]

In *The Adventures of Huckleberry Finn* by Mark Twain, Huck says: *"It made me shiver. And I about made up my mind to pray, and see if I couldn't try to quit being the kind of a boy I was and be better. So I kneeled down. But the words wouldn't come.*

"Why wouldn't they? It warn't no use to try and hide it from Him.... I knowed very well why they wouldn't come. It was because my heart warn't right; it was because I wasn't square; it was because I was playing double. I was letting on to give up sin, but always inside of me I was holding on to the biggest one of all. I was trying to make my mouth say I would do the right thing and the clean thing... but deep down in me I knowed it was a lie, and He knowed it. You can't pray a lie—I found that out."[48]

As Huck realized, you cannot say one thing to Heavenly Father and think and believe another. If our prayers are not sincere and honest, they will not ascend to heaven.

At times we may be so caught up in the mechanics of prayer that we drop into a routine. We say the same thing we always say, using the same words we always use, without giving our prayers much thought. The Lord calls this vain repetitions and counsels us, *"But when ye pray, use not vain repetitions, as the heathen do: for they think that they shall be heard for their much speaking."*[49]

Our words are vain because nothing is accomplished. It will do us no good to say the same thing over and over again without putting thought and feeling into what we are saying. When our prayers become shallow, trite, routine, or repetitive we are becoming too casual in our efforts to draw closer to Heavenly Father and are failing to show appropriate reverence and respect for our God.

It will also hinder our communication with God if, when we pray, we go on and on and think that if we have much to say every time we pray, it will be pleasing to our Father in Heaven. In Ecclesiastes we are told, *"Be not rash with thy mouth, and let not thine heart be hasty to utter any thing before God.... therefore let thy words be few...a fool's voice is known by multitude of words."*[50]

A friend of mine named Doug demonstrated just what can be done by offering a simple, sincere, and heartfelt prayer. He recounts, "Late one night a friend and I were leaving a scout camp located about fifteen miles up a winding mountain road. We had loaded the camping gear into the back of my pickup truck and headed for home, thinking we were the last to leave the camp.

"We hadn't traveled more than a couple of miles down the road when I felt a strange vibration, and about five seconds later I heard a loud clunk and then a dragging sound. This was not a welcome sound on such a dark road, barely wide enough for two cars to pass each other. Luckily, just ahead was one of the few pull-off areas on the road, so I coasted over to the side.

"As I got out and looked under the truck, there was just enough light reflecting off the hillside for me to see my driveline hanging down on the ground. I fumbled through my gear, found a flashlight, climbed under the truck, and confirmed that my universal joint had failed.

"We wondered what we should do since we were on a remote mountain road thirteen miles from town. Our wives were no doubt already concerned because we were not home yet. We thought about walking to town, but that would take too long. Besides, I didn't want to leave the truck with all our gear in it.

"We decided the only alternative left was to try and fix it. In order to do this, we would have to find the end cap and forty little roller bearings, each the size of a pencil lead and do it in the dark. We walked along the road looking for reflections in the moonlight. I reached down and picked up a tiny roller bearing and then another and another, but could not find enough to fix the car.

"I had tried to fix the car on my own and couldn't, so now in faith, I turned to God for help. I had prayed many times in the past and had great faith in prayers. I offered the following prayer;

'Dear Heavenly Father, thou knowest we are in a mess. Our families are worried about us and we need to get home. We need to fix the truck and thou knowest where the parts are to fix it. We have looked and haven't found all that we need. Please help us. I know we can do it with thy help. I ask this in the name of Jesus Christ. Amen.'

"Not more than five minutes later a car came down the road. It was a scout leader who had left the camp even later than we did. He had some tools, a good light, and a willing spirit. He backed up his car, and using his car's headlights, we discovered more of the roller bearings lying in the middle of the road. But it was still not enough. Then I received the inspiration to look elsewhere for something that was strong and thick enough to hold the end cap snug.

"It seemed impossible that we could find what we needed. But with Heavenly Father's help, the late-arriving, good-hearted scout leader found in the bottom of his tool box a piece of plumber's gasket material made of hard but flexible rubber. He had been carrying it in his toolbox for years, but never needed it. We cut a small strip, put it in the end cap, and slipped it over the universal joint. It held snugly.

"Only twenty minutes from the time I offered the prayer, we were on our way and reached our home without any other problems."

Our prayers do not have to be long or flowery, just sincere and offered in faith.

Are We Asking for the Right Thing?

Another reason that we might not receive an answer to our prayers is because we are praying for the wrong thing. We are praying for something a righteous, just, and fair God would not allow. We may pray to intervene in another person's life, for example, to turn a wayward child from his path of self-destruction.

This may be a perfectly noble and correct thing to pray for, but the Lord is not going to take away the freedom that he accords to each of his children, that is the right to choose for themselves what they will think and do. Each of us is given the opportunity to choose what we will do, be it right or wrong. Yes, we can pray that he will send assistance to try and support, counsel, or coach them, but the final decision is up to them.

We might also choose to pray for that which we know deep down in our heart is wrong. We might pray for something unkind to happen to another, or we may pray for things that a loving God knows would not be best for us. The apostle John puts it this way: *"And this is the confidence that we have in him, that, if we ask any thing **according to his will**, he heareth us."* [51] It is important to remember that when we go to our Father in Heaven in prayer, it should not be to try and change his mind, but to understand what he would like us to do.

Are We Ungrateful?

Do we continue to petition our Heavenly Father for more and more and never even acknowledge what our kind and generous Father in Heaven has already given us? If we do, then we may find ourselves in the same position that nine of the ten lepers were in after being healed by the Savior from the detestable and dreaded disease, leprosy. The nine never so much as uttered a "thank you" to the Lord, who had healed them from this agonizing illness that would have eventually killed them.

Failing to be grateful is not only disappointing to our Father in Heaven but it is also discourteous and selfish. Ingratitude will keep us from appreciating the many great and wonderful blessings that our generous Father has given us. And if it continues, it can lead to the loss of hope, humility, and happiness as well as the desire to communicate with Heavenly Father.

Are We Asking for Things that Don't Matter?

Sometimes we may ask God for an answer to a decision that is not important for us to receive. For example, we may ask our Father in Heaven to tell us which style of curtains we should hang in our house, what color car to buy, or what kind of flowers to plant in our yard.

Certainly these are the kind of decisions that God leaves to us. The process of growing, progressing, and gaining in wisdom and knowledge comes from the choices we make in life. If Heavenly Father made every decision for us, we would never grow and progress.

I remember meeting a young man a number of years ago who believed that he should take every decision to God, no matter how small. He believed if he did this, he would never have to make a mistake. I remember he told me that he even asked Heavenly Father whether he should have scrambled eggs or fried eggs for breakfast.

I also heard of another man who would take hours to go grocery shopping because he wanted to pray about which brand of food he should select for every item on his shopping list.

This kind of behavior is not only inappropriate and a waste of time, but it can affect our faith in prayer. We may mistakenly come to believe that God does not answer our prayers because this endless bombardment of inconsequential requests to heaven does not produce answers to our prayers.

A Prescription for Prayer

If we feel that we do not receive answers to our prayers as regularly as we would like to, then we may want to review the following list of actions that may make our prayers more meaningful.

❖ Be humble and reverent and remember that you are talking to our perfect and omnipotent Heavenly Father.

❖ Be willing to accept our Father in Heaven's will, regardless of the answer.

❖ Be focused, think about who you are praying to, and do not let your mind wander.

❖ Be patient, pause after you have finished talking, ponder, and wait for an answer to your prayer, but realize that God answers prayers in his own time frame.

❖ Be certain to pray directly to your Heavenly Father and not to anyone else.

❖ Be faithful and believe that God will answer your prayers as he has promised.

❖ Be prepared to work diligently to bring about what you have asked your Father in Heaven to help you accomplish, and do not expect God to do everything.

❖ Be sincere and honest in your petitions.

❖ Be thankful for the blessings you have received and express your gratitude to your Father in Heaven.

❖ Be submissive and seek to obtain only those things that Heavenly Father knows are best for you by ending your prayers with the statement, "I ask for these things, if it be thy will."

❖ Be sensible, ask for things that are right, and do not ask for frivolous things that do not really matter.

❖ Be prepared to pray for an answer to a major decision only after studying the alternatives, weighing the various choices, and then bringing your selected option to Heavenly Father to verify if you have chosen wisely.

❖ Be wise enough to ask God for the wisdom to know what to pray for.

❖ Be certain to close your prayers in the name of Jesus Christ.

Our kind and loving Father in Heaven wants us to pray to him, and he is most willing to answer our petitions. If our heart is right, then we will find that the windows of heaven will not be closed to us.

Chapter Seven

Turning to God in Time of Need

———•———

We should never think that the only reason we have hardships, challenges, or problems is because we have done something wrong. Every one of us will experience trials, disappointments, and pain before we complete our stay on the earth. It is the great equalizer. It is the process that can soften and humble us, make us more submissive to God, make us better people, and refine our character.

When we are in trouble, sad, or lonely, we should remember that our omnipotent Father in Heaven stands with open arms to welcome us. As Horatius

Bonar said, "In the day of prosperity, we have many refuges to resort to; in the day of adversity, only One."

A friend of mine, whom I will call Sara, tells of being in an extremely abusive environment while growing up in the Philippines and having no one to turn to but Father in Heaven. Sara's father beat her and her brothers. His cruelty included taking off his children's clothes and then hanging them by their necks so their feet were barely touching the floor. On occasion he would hang her brothers upside down and leave them in that position for hours. He also put one of her brothers in a sack and beat him with a belt buckle.

One day Sara's father chased her with a large kitchen knife, but she managed to escape by hiding in a neighbor's house. During the next two years, she went to live with her grandmother, who also believed in freely administering a depraved form of corporal punishment to her granddaughter.

When Sara was fourteen, she decided that she had to get away and went to live in Manila with her aunt. Here she was harassed and molested by her uncle, so she moved in with her other aunt, who was absolutely destitute and lived in a shantytown because she could not overcome her gambling addiction.

Sara had gone from one abusive home only to land in another and another. Now she found herself entangled in the midst of extreme poverty and living in a hovel. What was she to do? How could she liberate herself from this life of abuse and poverty and make something of herself? She felt so helpless and knew she lacked the wisdom to escape from this repugnant environment.

As she pondered what seemed like a hopeless situation, memories of the past came to her. She remembered as a small child learning the importance of praying to God when you find yourself in trouble. So one morning she got up and made her way to a nearby church. She found a quiet place inside where she could be alone and began to pray. She begged her Heavenly Father to help her find a better life. She prayed all day and then returned to do the same thing the next day. This lonely vigil continued for the rest of the week and into the next week and the next.

Then one day Sara was offered a chance to escape her deplorable living conditions. She was given work as a nanny for a family that would provide room and board and also pay her a salary. She was required to work seven days every week, but she was in a safe environment that gave her an opportunity to improve her lot in life.

As a young girl Sara learned a most valuable lesson. When those closest to you, the ones who are supposed to love and support you, fail, you can turn to your Heavenly Father who will always be there and will never let you down. Problems that seem insurmountable can be worked through when the power of God comes into your life.

Sara never stopped praying to her Heavenly Father, and she continued to progress. In time she was able to qualify for a better job working in a store. Although she still had trials and troubles along the way, she continued to grow and advance. Today she lives in affluence in the United States, and teaches her children to never forget the fact that we are children of God and he will never let us down if we will call on him for help.

By exercising her faith in God and focusing on serving other people, she was able to put aside the terrible memories of a violated childhood and find satisfaction and joy in serving others.

If we will pray to our loving and compassionate Father, he may not immediately remove all our pains and problems, but he will do what is best for us. He will answer our prayers and bless and help us according to the knowledge and wisdom of a perfect heavenly parent.

Although our Father in Heaven could easily remove every difficulty from our life, he will not do so, any more than we would remove every challenge or difficult task that comes into the lives of our children. We know that doing so would rob them of the opportunity to grow and progress.

Our Heavenly Father is a very attentive Parent, who deals with the smallest details pertaining to his children. If we respond appropriately to the challenges and trials in our lives, we will be softened, humbled, and refined in a way that will help us become more like Jesus Christ.

Jesus is the Role Model to Follow in Times of Crisis

If we examine the life of Jesus Christ, who served as a perfect teacher and our role model, we will see that he demonstrated what we should do in times of crisis.

1. Jesus turned to his Father in all things and did exactly what his Father had taught him. In the New Testament, in the book of John, we read, *"Then said Jesus unto them...I do nothing of myself; but as my Father hath taught me."*[52]

2. Jesus taught us to pray more earnestly when things become extremely difficult. When the Savior was in the Garden of Gethsemane in terrible pain, we learn what he did from the words of Luke: *"And being in agony he **prayed more earnestly**: and his sweat was as it were great drops of blood falling down to the ground."*[53]

3. Jesus prayed for what he wanted, but then did what the Father wanted. The Savior did not want to endure the most terrible pain and torture ever experienced by man, and he prayed to be able to forgo this ordeal. But regardless of what he wanted, he yielded to his Father's will. Luke records Jesus' words: *"... Father, if thou be willing,*

remove this cup from me: nevertheless not my will, but thine be done."[54]

4. Jesus did not become angry when his Father did not lift the burden from his shoulders. He who drank the bitterest cup in history did not become bitter.

    Trials can harden us or they can soften us, depending on how we respond to them. I remember hearing a Sunday School teacher tell of an experience he had with his teenage class while discussing the way various people handle their trials. One young lady said, "Boiling water hardens eggs and softens carrots." He thought this was a pretty silly thing to say until he thought about it more carefully and recognized the wisdom of this young lady. Some people become bitter and hardened when forced to deal with trials while others become humble and are able to grow from them.

    It is not what happens to us but how we respond to what happens to us that determines the measure of our character. If we respond the way Jesus Christ did, we will become more like him.

5. Jesus comforted and served others while he was experiencing terrible pain. During the final hours he spent in mortality, he was

not concentrating on his own problems but was instead focused on healing the severed ear of the servant of the high priest, forgiving the brutal soldiers who had mocked him, beaten him, and nailed him to the cross, reassuring the thief on the cross next to him, and ensuring that his mother would be cared for after he was gone. But what is truly amazing is that he did all this while in the traumatic and agonizing process of suffering for the sins of all mankind and opening the way for us to live with God forever.

6. Jesus endured to the end. He did this by praying to know what he should do and then doing it. And he did it by serving others without reservation or complaint in spite of his own trials.

When We Take Our Problems to Heavenly Father

Heavenly Father May Lift Some of Our Burdens Immediately

When we take our problems to Father in Heaven, sometimes he will respond by immediately lifting those burdens from our shoulders. One day, while I was working in the garage, I climbed up a ladder to place some boxes on a shelf. As I was ascending the ladder, I jammed my head into the sharp end of the sheet metal bracing that held the garage door in place. I cut open the top of my head and soon had blood running down my face.

As my wife, Carolee rushed me to the emergency room of the hospital, I prayed for relief and comfort. My prayers were answered immediately, and I remember being at peace as I sat in the emergency room while the doctor sewed up my head. I was comforted during the ordeal, and no permanent damage resulted from this accident. My prayers were immediately answered.

Another example of a prayer being immediately answered took place in the life of a lady named Robin. Her son had been frugal and saved $237 to buy two tickets for her and her husband to go to a special concert. From the Christmas morning that Robin received this gift until the day of the concert on March 17th, she looked forward with great anticipation to the coming of the special event.

However, during the intervening period, Robin suffered some rather serious health challenges, and on one visit to the doctor he informed her that she would need surgery and the only day available was March 17th. She did not want to disappoint her son, but at the same time she realized the importance of obtaining the surgery as soon as possible to keep her health problem from becoming life threatening. She did not know what to do as it took a long time and some difficulty to get the surgical appointment in the first place. So she decided to turn it over to God and prayed for help. Shortly thereafter, the doctor called and said, "The date of your surgery has been moved from the 17th to the 24th." Yes, Heavenly Father once again came to the rescue and helped work through this little problem that had large emotional consequences.

God is aware of the details. He knows what is happening in our life, and he can and often does intervene when we ask for help. Although he may not answer all our prayers immediately, God understands better than we do when receiving an immediate answer is essential.

A number of years ago, my wife, Carolee and I were traveling across the desert. Road conditions were very poor as a result of cold and snowy weather. Carolee was driving when suddenly the car hit a patch of black ice. It spun around on the ice until it was pointed directly at the oncoming traffic in the fast lane and then died. Instantly we pleaded with Heavenly Father to help us before another car came down that same patch of icy freeway and caused a head-on collision. As we prayed, we frantically worked to start the car and were able to get it going, turned around, and out of danger.

Although each of these challenges was of short duration, each resulted in prayers being offered and immediately answered. These experiences also resulted in the petitioner drawing closer to, and having greater love for, our Heavenly Father.

God May Not Lift Our Burdens for a Season

There will be times when we pray for relief from our hardships, but it does not come immediately. Sometimes our Heavenly Father allows us to struggle with our challenges for a time because he knows the encounter will strengthen us and teach us. Phillips Brooks captures this sentiment in the following poem:

> O, do not pray for easy lives,
> Pray to be stronger men.
> Do not pray for tasks equal to your powers.
> Pray for powers equal to your tasks.[55]

We can take solace in the fact that God will not suffer us to be tested or tempted above what we are able to bear. The apostle Paul stated: "...*God is faithful, who will not suffer you to be tempted above that ye are able; but will with the temptation also make a way to escape that ye may be able to bear*." [56]

A friend of mine shared the experience her daughter, whom we shall call Kathleen, had a few years ago. She worked, saved, and sacrificed to buy a very expensive leather coat at Nordstrom. This was an extraordinary purchase in a family where hand-me-downs, not new leather coats, were the norm. Kathleen was delighted with her purchase, but once she arrived home, she found a small flaw in the coat.

She didn't want to return it because there were no more like it in the store; so she decided to keep it.

A few weeks after the new school year had begun, Kathleen briefly left her coat on a school bench and someone stole it. She was heartsick! After much searching and many tears, her family made it a matter of prayer. Weeks went by and they continued to pray, but there was no sign of the coat. Kathleen asked her mother if she thought a leather coat was important enough to pray about. Her mother assured her that God had heard her prayers and advised her to give it some time and not to lose hope.

Many months passed. Then one day, Kathleen walked into a classroom and saw a girl wearing her leather coat. She knew her approach must be careful and that she must not embarrass or accuse. Privately, she told the girl the coat was hers and that she could prove it by identifying the small flaw in the coat. At first, the girl was unwilling to listen, but eventually she agreed to return the coat. Kathleen's faith had been tested, but she never gave up hope, and after a season her prayers were answered.

The periods in our lives when growth occurs most rapidly are not the most pleasant and comfortable ones. They are the times when we must endure, hold on, and continue to climb the insurmountable summits. These are the periods in our life when we must replace fear with faith and gain a witness that, with God's help, we *can* endure and overcome our challenges, no matter what is required. When we look back on this life, we will see that these periods of stress and hardship were the periods when the greatest growth occurred and the most progress was made in refining our character and increasing our capabilities and confidence. Heavenly Father will provide the opportunities for every one of us to be tested and tried. Not even the apostles of Jesus Christ were exempted.

Jesus, after teaching and feeding more than five thousand people in the rural area near the Sea of Galilee, directed his apostles to board a boat and head out towards Capernaum. Apparently he planned to meet with them en route at the city of Bethsaida, where they could continue the journey together by boat.[57]

Once the apostles had launched their boats onto the Sea of Galilee, a violent storm arose that kept them from being able to make much progress. In fact, after laboring at the oars for eight to ten hours, they had only been able to travel about twenty-five or thirty furlongs, (three-and-a-half miles). Then, when things seemed the darkest, during the fourth watch of the night (between three and six a.m.),[58] Jesus came to the apostles walking on the water. It is interesting to note that Jesus did not come to them until they had labored and struggled against the terrifying storm for most of the night.

How discouraged the apostles must have been as they struggled and pulled against the waves for so long in the pitch-black night. How exhausted, helpless, and alone they must have felt, lost in the vastness of the black and stormy sea. I can just imagine how they must have pleaded with their Heavenly Father to save them and protect them from the threatening storm that could overwhelm and destroy them.

Then in the darkest part of the night, Jesus came to them walking on the water, and they heard that wonderful greeting from the greatest source of light in the world: *"Be of good cheer: it is I; be not afraid."*[59] This same message is not for the weary despairing disciples alone but is for all of us who struggle to overcome the trials of life.

Yes, the apostles were saved, but not until they had struggled and toiled for many hours. We might ask the question, "Why would the apostles be required to endure for so many hours in this horrifying environment before they were rescued?" I believe the answer is clear: this experience strengthened them and helped them realize that they were not alone, that their petitions were heard, and that they were beloved children of our Father in Heaven. It also reminded them of their dependency upon the Lord and that the same power used to still the terrifying wind and waves would be used to bless their lives when needed

Some Burdens Are Not Taken From Us in This Life

Some problems we pray to have taken from us will never leave us in mortality. Individuals that have diseases like diabetes, arthritis, or a terminal illness will likely carry these burdens for the remainder of their lives.

You may ask, "If Heavenly Father is not going to remove these challenges from my life, why should I even bother to pray about them?" We need to pray for strength to bear our burdens well and for the comfort from the Holy Spirit that reminds us that we are not required to endure these problems alone. As the 19th century English preacher C. H. Spurgeon said, *"As sure as ever God puts his children in the furnace, he will be in the furnace with them."*[60]

I have a friend named Pat who has one of these life-long challenges. She suffers from diabetes. Her health is very unstable, and sometimes she has to fight off one affliction after another for months. One day when she was praying about this condition, inspiration came into her mind. She was told that she would never be left alone, that she would have a support system that would be there to help her whenever she needed it.

She said, "On occasion I have to be reminded of this when I start feeling down because sometimes I feel very alone. So in the depth of my loneliness and despair, I pray and ask my Heavenly Father for help."

Our loving Heavenly Father understands! He is compassionate and caring and does not want us to suffer. But he wants what is best for us, and he knows that what is best is not always what is easy. Some of the character development classes we are required to enroll in during this life are not necessarily pleasant and are certainly not ones we would have chosen as electives if we had been given a choice.

Consider for a moment the life of Paul the apostle. In a letter he wrote to the Corinthians, Paul states, *"...five times received I forty stripes save one. Thrice was I beaten with rods, once was I stoned, thrice I suffered shipwreck, a night and a day I have been in the deep. In journeyings often, in perils of waters, in perils of robbers, in perils by my own countrymen, in perils by the heathen, in perils in the city, in perils in the wilderness, in perils in the sea, in perils among false brethren; In weariness and painfulness, in watchings often, in hunger and thirst, in fastings often, in cold and nakedness."*[61]

He not only had to endure many severe trials in his life, but he had one problem plaguing him that he was required to endure for the rest of his life. He says, *"...there was given to me a thorn in the flesh...For this thing I besought the Lord thrice, that it might depart from me."*[62] He prayed three times for relief, and I assume that this was not three prayers that were offered, but three seasons of prayers. The answer he received to his prayers was, *"My grace is sufficient for thee: for my strength is made perfect in weakness."*[63]

What is remarkable here is that after all Paul suffered and endured to teach and serve, he was still required to bear this burden; it would not be lifted from him. However, what is even more extraordinary is Paul's response to his denied petition, *"Therefore I take pleasure in infirmities, in reproaches, in necessities, in persecutions, in distresses for Christ's sake: for when I am weak, then am I strong."*[64] Are we able to respond with a cheerful heart when Heavenly Father does not lift our burdens?

Paul had the wisdom to know that it is in times of need and weakness that we can feel the closest to our Heavenly Father, and that this is when the most growth takes place. The Old Testament story of Shadrach, Meshach, and Abed-nego demonstrates this also.

When Nebuchadnezzar was the king of Babylon, he created a 90-foot golden image and commanded everyone to bow down and worship it. Shadrach, Meshach, and Abed-nego refused to do it because they knew there was only one true God, and he had forbidden the worship of idols.

When Nebuchadnezzar heard that these three men, to whom he had given positions of authority in the government, refused to yield to his will, he became furious. He called them in and gave them another chance. Perhaps at this point they could have rationalized that if they did what the king wanted, they would not be put to death and would live to be able to accomplish much good in the future. But they did not compromise their principles and honor. In fact, their courageous and faithful response to the king is marvelous: *"O Nebuchadnezzar, we are not careful to answer thee in this matter. If it be so, our God whom we serve is able to deliver us from the burning fiery furnace, and he will deliver us out of thine hand, O king. But if not, be it known unto thee, O king, that we will not serve thy gods, nor worship the golden image which thou hast set up."*[65] Then the scriptures tell us that the king was *"full of fury"*[66] and commanded that the furnace be heated to seven times as hot as it would normally be heated and commanded the *"most mighty men that were in his army to bind Shadrach, Meshach and Abed-nego and to cast them into the burning fiery furnace."* [67]

These three faithful followers of God were only doing what they knew was right and certainly did not want to be burned to death. I am sure they prayed mightily for their lives to be spared. If we stopped right at this point, we might assume that their prayers were not answered, because they were thrown into the fiery furnace.

If we did stop here, we might even question why a loving and compassionate God would allow this to happen to them. After all, didn't he love them? Hadn't he promised that if we ask for that which is right, it would be given to us? Hadn't they been righteous? Weren't they asking for that which was right? Didn't they show great faith and courage by acknowledging the fact that they knew God could save them, but if he didn't, they still would not bow down and worship the idol?

You might ask, "Does this situation apply to me today? If I pray for relief and my burdens are not lifted, do I question God, doubt myself, or become angry or bitter? In my state of depression, would I further question my Heavenly Father's motives? Could God have answered their prayers so that maybe they could have been left in jail instead of being cast into the furnace? Could Heavenly Father have spared them the anxiety and emotional trauma of having to be delivered at the point of death?"

The answer to these last questions is, of course, he could! However, we need to understand that this is not the end of the story. If we stopped here, we would never reach the glorious end. In spite of their prayers, Shadrach, Meshach, and Abed-nego were cast into a super-heated furnace. But God's ways are not our ways and his thoughts are higher and better than ours. And because they were thrown into the furnace, they were able to see in their own lives the divine and miraculous power of God to bless and protect them. They were given the sacred privilege of visiting with the Son of God.

Their faith must have become unshakable as they were eventually delivered from the fiery furnace that was so hot that it had killed the men who threw them into the inferno. Shadrach, Meshach, and Abed-nego came forth from the flames without even the odor of the fire on their clothes. As they stepped out of the furnace, Nebuchadnezzar, the king, honored them, gave them the freedom to worship unmolested, promised to protect them from their detractors, and promoted them to influential positions in the government.

Not only were their lives blessed, but a great many other people were also benefited from this experience. It gave hope to all who saw the miracle occur or who later heard about it. This miracle may have caused some to turn to God and others to renew their efforts to live a more righteous life and draw closer to Heavenly Father. And Nebuchadnezzar proclaimed by decree that no one, upon threat of their lives, could ever speak against the God of Shadrach, Meshach and Abed-nego.[68]

Do we sometimes find ourselves deep in despair and caught up in the midst of a challenge, hardship, or problem that has come into our lives? We pray for relief and no relief seems to come. We question ourselves and wonder why our request is not granted, and in time we might even begin to question God. He has promised to answer our prayers. Why won't he lift this burden from me? It is not fair. I have tried to live a good life, so why is this happening to me?

C. S. Lewis comments on the fact that we sometimes resist God's attempt to make more out of us than we can make of ourselves. He says, "Imagine yourself as a living house. God comes in to rebuild that house. At first, perhaps, you can understand what He is doing. He is getting the drains right and stopping the leaks in the roof and so on; you know that those jobs needed doing and so you are not surprised. But presently he starts knocking the house about in a way that hurts abominably and does not seem to make sense.

"What on earth is He up to? The explanation is that He is building quite a different house from the one you thought of—throwing out a new wing here, putting on an extra floor there, running up towers, making courtyards. You thought you were going to be made into a decent little cottage, but He is building a palace. He intends to come and live in it Himself."[69]

We must come to understand that all sincere prayers are heard by a loving Heavenly Father, who wants what is best for us, and that he will respond in a way that will most help us. If Heavenly Father wants us to continue to carry the burden we have been given, then we might ask him to strengthen us to be able to bear up under the load more easily. We may ask for peace and the Spirit of God to comfort us and let us know that we are not alone.

We may recognize that we could never appreciate the joy of success if we have never struggled and overcome. We could not truly understand the sweet if we never experienced the bitter. We could not enjoy eternal joy and happiness without tasting of disappointment and hardship. And how could we really have an appreciation of what it is like to live forever without pain or disease if we had never suffered, been ill, or tasted of death?

And finally we must realize that even if we are required to carry our burdens until we leave mortality, this life is not the last act in the drama of life. If we remember Shadrach, Meshach and Abed-nego's story, it did not end when they were in the furnace. It ended with a triumphant exit from the flames and the bestowal of great blessings upon their heads. So will it be with us. There is great reason for hope for a glorious future when we will be free of pain, distress, and disappointment. If we continue to call upon Heavenly Father in prayer and endure in faith and courage to the end, one day we will hear the Savior and our Heavenly Father say to us, "Well done," and God will shower us with greater blessings than we can possibly imagine.

Chapter Eight

Protecting Your Family in a Dangerous World

—•—

*T*he opening line in Charles Dickens' *A Tale of Two Cities* states, *"It was the best of times, it was the worst of times, it was the age of wisdom, it was the age of foolishness...it was the season of Light, it was the season of Darkness, it was the spring of hope, it was the winter of despair...."*[70]

Although these lines were penned nearly 150 years ago, they seem to be an accurate description of our day. Never in the history of the world has the human family had so much. Never has knowledge been as great or information so abundant. In the past, humanity drank in knowledge drop by drop; now it comes so fast it is like trying to drink from a fire hose.

Never have there been so many inventions to ease our burdens and increase our opportunities. Medical discoveries are being made at an unprecedented rate to protect and prolong our lives. We can travel across the world more quickly and in greater comfort than ever before in the history of the world. We can also view the world instantly through the countless websites that are now available over the Internet.

Nevertheless, many question whether or not we are better off today. We just need to pick up any newspaper to read about terrorist attacks killing innocent people, senseless acts of violence, drive-by shootings, school shootings, parents killing their children, and a countless list of other horrible crimes.

Pornography is one of the biggest money makers through the pervasive showcasing of its vile wares; gambling is growing in popularity as it takes precious dollars from paychecks that should be feeding families; drugs have become an epidemic that enslave so many and destroy countless lives; dishonesty has permeated business, sports, government, journalism, and medicine; and immorality is becoming the accepted standard in our society.

Truly we are in that period of time foretold by Paul when he said, "...*perilous times shall come. For men shall be lovers of their own selves, covetous, boasters, proud, blasphemers, disobedient to parents, unthankful, unholy, without natural affection...lovers of pleasure more than lovers of God....*"[71]

Natural and manmade disasters that kill thousands of people each year are increasing at an alarming rate. Through the wonders of the media, we also track the impact of the many wars and hostilities that rage across the world. In the 24th chapter of Matthew, Jesus talked about our time when these conditions would prevail. He said, *"And ye shall hear of wars and rumors of wars...For nation shall rise against nation, and kingdom against kingdom: and there shall be famines, and pestilences, and earthquakes, in divers places...And because iniquity shall abound, the love of many shall wax cold."*[72]

What are we to do in order to live, thrive, and prosper in this troubled world? The apostle Paul says, *"For God hath not given us the spirit of fear; but of power, and of love, and of a sound mind."*[73]

Paul also tells us how to protect ourselves in these days: *"Wherefore take unto you the whole armour of God, that ye may be able to stand in the evil day, and having done all, to stand...Praying always with all prayer and supplication in the Spirit...."*[74]

If we are to protect our families and ourselves then we must do as Paul advises and pray.

Personal Prayers

I believe that each of us should begin the day by kneeling down and saying a personal prayer. It should be offered in a place where we can be alone to quietly pour out the feelings of our heart to our Heavenly Father. This may be the most important prayer we offer all day because it gives us the opportunity to ask for assistance in all that we have to do during the day. After you finish expressing gratitude, ask yourself, "What do I have to do today that I could do more effectively if Heavenly Father were helping me?" Then pray accordingly.

Personal prayers can and should be offered throughout the day as occasion requires. We can pray wherever we are and as many times as we desire. We can pray quietly without anyone knowing it. We can pray for wisdom, help, protection, comfort, insight, judgment, tenderness, charity, or whatever we may need. Throughout my life, I have found that things always go better with prayer.

One morning a friend of mine named Zenny offered a personal prayer to try and overcome the distress and sadness she was feeling as she mourned for the loss of her companion who had died a few days before. She asked her Heavenly Father to bless her and give her comfort and peace. After she finished praying, she felt that she wanted to go upstairs to the master bedroom in their house.

She had not been able to enter this room since her husband had died in his sleep from a heart attack. Now she was prompted to enter the room and go over to the television and turn it on. As soon as the television came on, she saw a man giving a talk. He said, "If you have lost a friend or a loved one, do not despair, for you are not alone. Your Heavenly Father and Savior, Jesus Christ, will be with you and comfort you and bring peace to you."

Immediately she felt a wave of warmth and peace come over her, and she felt comforted and calm. She could feel the love and caring of her Heavenly Father and knew that He had heard her prayer and immediately answered it.

No matter how often we may pray during the day, it is always good to offer another personal prayer before we go to bed. It allows us to check in and report to our Father in Heaven on how we did during the day.

When one of my daughters was little, she wanted to set up her bed in the room where she could watch a video before she fell asleep. I found a video that she wanted to watch, her mother made up the bed for her, and we kissed her good night. As we were walking out of the room, she said, "Daddy, will you check back and make sure that I am all right?"

I believe that many of us want this same kind of relationship with our Heavenly Father. I know there are times in my life when I feel like saying to my Father in Heaven, "Will you check back and make sure that I am all right?" We draw closer to Heavenly Father as we confide our innermost feelings to him and express our love for him and listen to the still small voice reassure us that he loves us.

Another thing I have found to be helpful in our family is for my wife and me to kneel beside our bed just before we go to sleep and say a prayer together. It is most difficult for an argument or a disagreement to continue into the next day if we humbly express our love for our spouse before we retire for the night.

Teaching Our Children to Pray

If personal prayers are important for us, then certainly they are important for our children. We have the responsibility to teach our children to communicate with their Father in Heaven. It is reassuring to read the words in Proverbs that counsel us to, *"Train up a child in the way he should go: and when he is old, he will not depart from it"*[75]

We can begin to teach them as soon as they are able to kneel and talk to their Heavenly Father by saying a few words that they can repeat after us, such as,

"Dear Heavenly Father, thank you for our family. I ask you to bless me and Mommy and Daddy. I love you. In the name of Jesus Christ, Amen."

As our children mature, the content and scope of their prayers should expand to take into consideration the needs of others besides their immediate family.

A friend once told me of an experience she had with one of her little children named Lizzie, who was just learning to pray. She had learned to pray by repeating the prayers her mother voiced for her. In time, she was able to say her prayers unaided. But one day, when her mother asked her to say her prayers, she said, "Will you help me?" Then she immediately started to pray without waiting for her mother to tell her what to say. However, this time she wanted her mother to repeat the words she said. It does not take long for most children to learn to pray, and we can learn from them as we listen to them exercise their wonderful child-like faith.

We need to serve as role models for our children by continuing to call upon Heavenly Father for assistance and to give thanks for the endless blessings that most surely will be ours for the asking. We might ask ourselves, "When was the last time my children saw me praying?" When our children are young, they will want to emulate the things they see their parents do.

One day when my wife and I were working in the yard, our little daughter came running from the house screaming. She had swallowed a candy and felt she was choking. We took her into the house and had her drink some water, but she continued to be upset. Through her tears she said, "Daddy, say a prayer for me." I stopped and said a prayer with her, and within a few moments she calmed down and all was well. It was gratifying to see this child-like faith demonstrated in a moment of crisis.

Some parents think they should wait to teach their children about prayer until they are old enough to make up their own minds about religion. I think this is a serious mistake, as they would be depriving their children of the countless blessings that a loving and generous God will bestow upon them as they are growing up. If your children do not pray, they will not be able to develop the close relationship with their Heavenly Father that can bring peace, comfort, and confidence into their lives as they come to understand that they are beloved children of God. As Isaiah said so many years ago, *"And all thy children shall be taught of the Lord, and great shall be the peace of thy children."*[76]

A few months ago I heard a 17-year-old girl named Abby giving a talk in church on the topic of prayer. I was amazed at the wisdom of this young lady. She said, "Think about how you feel when you take the time to pray with a sincere heart and truly have the desire to be in tune with the Holy Spirit. Those sweet moments of peace that I feel change the way I think about myself and what I believe my relationship is to Heavenly Father.

"Knowing that he hears my prayers and wants to be a part of my life affects the way I treat others and how I go about my day. How wonderful it would be to have those feelings always as we keep a prayer in our heart. I can think of no greater blessing. I am so pleased that there are no quotas on the number of prayers we can have, no time limits on how long we can pray, and no electronic breakdowns to worry about. We can pray always."

Once a child is taught to pray, he or she will not only be able to bring the power of God down into his or her own life but will also be able to bless the lives of the entire family.

This was exactly the situation that took place in Shelby's house when she was about five years old. Her father had been working out of town five days a week for several years. She missed her father a great deal, so one day she decided she was going to do something about it. She knelt and prayed,

"Dear Heavenly Father, please bless us that Daddy will be able to come home and visit us."

Later that night Shelby's mother called and told Dad about this touching prayer. After Shelby's father hung up the phone, feelings began to stir within him. Yes, he knew he was gone from home far too much. He was not doing what he knew he should do to be with his family and to help them as they were growing up. Nevertheless, he felt torn because he loved his job and really appreciated his coworkers. He also realized that with his limited schooling, it would be difficult to find another job that would pay as well.

Nevertheless, Heavenly Father had heard the sweet, humble prayer of his little daughter, and things began to happen. Not long after Shelby's prayer was uttered, her dad was called into his boss's office and told that they were restructuring the company and that his position had been eliminated. He was offered a nice severance package, and within two weeks he found another job that allowed him to be home every day. The sincere prayer offered by a young child helped bless her entire family.

One of the vacations our children enjoy the most is traveling to Disneyland. Last year, we planned a trip and ordered passes over the Internet several months before the much-anticipated date. We purchased four-day passes for each member of the family which cost several hundred dollars, a significant sum for our family.

When the day came that we were to leave on vacation, I remembered the passes and thought I had better not forget to pack them. I went to retrieve them from the place where I kept them, but they were not there. I spent the next hour looking for them in every conceivable place I could imagine.

I shared my anxiety with my little daughter. She looked at me in a very serious manner, and we talked and decided to ask Heavenly Father to help us find the passes. She and I knelt down and prayed to our Father in Heaven and asked him to help us find the missing passes. Immediately after arising from our prayer, the thought came to me to look in the top drawer of my desk.

As I followed this inspiration, I realized that I had been looking for the passes themselves instead of an envelope that contained the passes. I had mistakenly believed that I had removed them from the envelope when it had arrived weeks before and placed them in the customary place in my dresser drawer. However, as I searched through the material in my desk drawer, I found an envelope that contained the missing passes. They were located in less than a minute after we concluded our prayer, thanks to the faith of our little daughter.

Teaching children to pray when they are little will pay big dividends when they become teenagers. For example, I heard an experience a few days ago when a teenage boy and girl got into a car to go on a date. After they had fastened their seat belts, he asked his date, "Do you want to offer a prayer, or should I?"

What a great blessing it is when teenagers develop the faith that Heavenly Father will help them if they pray. A teenage girl named Carolyn shared the following story.

"I can remember an experience I had with prayer years ago that truly strengthened my faith in prayer. I had been given the responsibility of caring for my neighbors' cat while they were away on vacation.

"I had made sure to feed, clean, and care for the cat to the best of my abilities. But one day, late at night, the black cat leaped through my legs as I stepped out the door, only to be swallowed up by the darkness. I was devastated. The cat was not supposed to be let outside. I searched for the cat for hours, calling him, setting out warm milk, and listening intently for the bell on his collar. With tears in my eyes, I folded my arms and began to pray one of the most heartfelt prayers I have ever said.

"I know Heavenly Father heard my prayer that night because as I was ending my prayer, I heard a faint jingle and then saw two beady green eyes staring up at me. I was overwhelmed with joy and gratitude. I will be forever thankful to my Heavenly Father for helping me that night and for giving me that experience because it was the first time I saw the immediate effects of prayer."

If we have older children who have never been taught to pray, we might consider the following experience that was shared with me by a friend of mine named Dale. He was given the assignment to teach a group of 12-year-old boys about prayer. He and his wife talked about it over dinner the night before. They wondered how best to teach these young men why something as intangible as prayer was so important. They continued to discuss it that evening, and the next day Dale came to class armed with some large pieces of cardboard, a handkerchief, and some large candy bars.

He began his class by asking how many of the boys wanted a large candy bar. The vote was unanimous; they all wanted one. Next, he laid down the large cardboard squares in a random pattern on the floor of the classroom. Then he told them that anyone who could successfully navigate his way across the room while blindfolded, without stepping off of the cardboard squares and onto the carpet, would earn a candy bar. If they stepped off the squares and touched the carpet, they would be disqualified.

He also told them before starting that there was one way in which they could be assured of success but they would have to figure that out for themselves as it was the key to achieving their goal.

Then one by one he blindfolded them, turned them around in circles until they lost their bearings and each young man took a turn trying to cross the room without stepping off the cardboard squares to retrieve a candy bar. However, none of the boys successfully crossed the room without stepping off the cardboard squares.

Then Dale asked the young men if they could think of any way that they could get from one side of the room to the other without stepping on the carpet. He explained that crossing the room was like trying to overcome the hurdles and avoid the pitfalls on the road of life.

One of the young men suggested that if Dale would help them, they could successfully cross the room without stepping off the cardboard squares. So he allowed them to try again, but this time they could ask him for guidance as to the direction they should go and where they should step. Even though it was not easy, each of the blindfolded young men found that with Dale's guidance, they could successfully cross the room without stepping on the carpet and win their reward.

Then Dale explained to the boys that this is the way it is in life. If we ask our Heavenly Father for help and guidance, he will help us to successfully navigate our way through life.

Family Prayer

One of the most important things we can do to protect and help our family members through trouble, turmoil, and evil that they must face in the world today is to kneel as a family, both morning and evening, and ask for Heavenly Father's inspiration, protection, and direction. In Matthew, the Savior reminds us, *"For where two or three are gathered together in my name, there am I in the midst of them."*[77]

Family prayer not only allows us to unite our faith in sending our petitions to heaven, it brings us together as a family. Each time we pray, one member of the family serves as the voice in offering the prayer. It gives the person offering the prayer that day the chance to show love and concern for other members of the family.

If a family member is facing a particular challenge, it is appropriate to ask Heavenly Father to assist them with that particular concern as well as to ask for assistance to be given to all members of the family and others outside the family. A friend of mine named Wendy tells the story about how family prayer helped her son, Michael.

When he was 11 years old, Michael was walking around with his parakeet riding on his shoulder.

However, on this day he stepped outside the house, having forgotten that the bird, which they called "Bird," was on his shoulder. Bird flew off his shoulder and was gone. Michael ran into the house and urgently called the family together to have a family prayer to help him find his bird. Afterwards, everyone got off their knees and went outside to help look for the escapee.

After a while, Michael thought he heard his bird in a neighbor's yard. He went over to investigate, and sure enough, there was Bird. He was stuck in a thorn bush, and a cat was bearing down on him. In fact the cat had already bitten Bird's wing. Bird was rescued and taken to the veterinarian's office and eventually made a full recovery.

This is an example of a young man's faith in the power of family prayer and a demonstration of the fact that Father in Heaven hears and answers family prayers "where two [or more] are gathered in his name."

I can remember when our children were very young and, as we would kneel for family prayer, they would call out items they wanted included in the prayer, such as "Bless me," "Bless Mrs. Laredo," (a kindergarten teacher), "Bless Grandma," etc. Although this seemed a little unusual, we appreciated it because it showed their faith and their willingness to be involved in the prayer.

If you have small children, keep your kneeling family prayers short. If your prayers are long and drawn out, your little children will come to dislike praying. It is important to give little children an opportunity to be the voice from time to time during family prayer. When the children are very young, they may need to repeat the words of their parents until they are old enough to offer their own prayers.

One day before we left on a family trip, we knelt in family prayer and asked for Heavenly Father to protect us on our journey and help us to get to our destination and return home safely. Little thought was given to this petition afterward until we were traveling down a rural freeway about 75 miles an hour and suddenly saw a huge sheep standing in the middle of the freeway. When you are traveling at over 100 feet per second, it does not allow much time to react to an emergency.

We hoped that the sheep would not panic and run in front of the car as we tried to skirt around him. We could see that this sheep was so large that if we collided, not only would it result in the demise of the animal but it could also injure or kill members of our family. But, thanks to the protective mantle of heaven that came as a result of our family prayer that morning, the sheep did not move an inch as we safely flashed past it.

Praying before Meals

Another opportunity for the family to pray is when they sit down to eat. Giving thanks and asking for a blessing on the food helps us to show appreciation for what we have and reminds us that we need to be fed spiritually as well as physically.

I remember talking to a couple who had not been attending church for years and never mentioned anything to do with religion in their home. They had a son born to them whom they named Jackson, and he was a delight to them.

One day, when Jackson was almost three years old, the family was sitting at the dinner table getting ready to eat. Suddenly he announced, "We should pray."

They were astonished, for never had the subject ever come up in their house. Never had the word prayer ever been used. How could this little one know about prayer, and what were these feelings he was having? The parents just sat at the table in amazement as Jackson began to pray aloud. This extraordinary experience eventually led to his parents attending church and teaching Jackson to pray, something that was important but that had been overlooked in their home for too many years.

In the troubled world in which we live, we need to take the most important step we can take to provide safety, direction, and protection for our family members by kneeling in family and individual prayer.

We would not let our children go out in a storm without the protection of a coat, and we should not let them leave the house without the protective influence of prayer. Prayer has been removed from the schools, but we must make sure it is never removed from the most important school on earth, the home.

Chapter Nine

Prayer and Fasting

————•————

*S*ometimes when what we are praying for is extremely important to us, we may want to show greater sincerity in our petitions by fasting. We fast by voluntarily going without food or drink for a period of time. Fasting can be used to express earnestness and gratitude and to increase spirituality and humility. When we add fasting to our prayers, we are demonstrating a willingness to sacrifice for a time in order to show the sincerity of our petitions.

One of the objectives of prayer and fasting is to set aside the wants and needs of the body in order to draw closer to the things of the spirit and the promptings of the still, small voice. Fasting and prayer allow us to humble ourselves and recognize our dependence on Heavenly Father and the fact that we are totally reliant on him for all we have.

Turning to God in Time of Need

There are times when the wisdom of the world fails us, so we turn to God in fasting and prayer to do for us what we are unable to do for ourselves. Such was the case of a faithful family who turned to their Father in Heaven through fasting and prayer in a time of great travail.

It all began when the mother of the family, Joanna, suddenly experienced a trembling in her body and felt so weak she could not stand up. She was immediately taken to the doctor, who determined that her blood pressure had spiked to a dangerously high level that could have caused a stroke or heart attack. But this is where their diagnosis ended. They did not know why this had happened, nor could they prescribe medication to keep these episodes from recurring.

After this problem continued to recur for about six weeks, it was clear that medical science did not have the answers that were so urgently needed and earnestly sought. So her family and friends turned to a higher source and decided to fast and pray for her.

Although this did not result in a miraculous healing, it did give Joanna the strength and courage to continue to participate in what seemed like an unending series of tests and other medical procedures. It also helped her to deal more effectively with the terrible disappointment of knowing that not one of the many doctors she had seen could explain what she had or why it was happening.

During the next fifteen-month period, she continued to have almost daily occurrences when her blood pressure would shoot up without the slightest warning. After conducting every conceivable test, the doctors still had no idea what was causing this condition, nor had they ever seen anything like it before.

Then one day, after Joanna suffered a severe attack at her in-laws' house, the family decided that they needed to turn to God again. This time about 40 members of their family participated in fasting and praying for her. Everyone in her extended family wanted to participate, including Joanna's 5-year-old granddaughter, who chose to miss one meal as her fast so she could help her grandma.

The results of this fast were remarkable! Suddenly, after having experienced over one hundred encounters, the attacks stopped! The chief physician, our Heavenly Father, provided the much needed respite from the continuous waves of affliction, stress, and worry that had worn upon the soul of this sweet and loving lady for so long.

Yes, Heavenly Father wants us to experience trials and hardships that will build, strengthen, and refine us; but as a wise parent, he also knows when to lift the burdens.

Fasting has long been used by those who believe in our Father in Heaven and who want to draw closer to him. In the Old Testament, we read about the people of God fasting, and we know that both Moses and Elijah fasted for extended periods of time.[78]

One of the truly marvelous women mentioned in the Old Testament was Esther, the adopted daughter of Mordecai, who was Jewish. She was selected to be the queen to Ahasuerus, king of Persia.

One of the chief officers to the king was a man named Haman, who hated Mordecai because he would not show obeisance to Haman. He sought revenge against Mordecai for not bowing to him. Through deceit and manipulation, Haman obtained a decree from the king to put all the Jewish people in the kingdom to death on an assigned day.

Mordecai let Queen Esther know of the pending death decree and asked her to go to the king and plead for the lives of his people. However, there was a problem. In those days, if anyone went in unto the king without being invited, they could be put to death. Esther told Mordecai that the king had not sent for her to come unto him for thirty days and felt that to go in unannounced would be jeopardizing her life. However, since there was so much at stake, she decided that she would go in unto the king without an invitation. In preparation for this visit to the king, Esther sent the following message to Mordecai: *"Go, gather together all the Jews that are present in Shushan, and fast ye for me, and neither eat nor drink three days, night or day: I also and my maidens will fast likewise; and I go in unto the king, which is not according to the law: and if I perish, I perish."*[79]

The fasting and prayers of Esther and the people not only resulted in the king receiving her, although she was uninvited, but he also granted unto her anything she asked for, up to half the kingdom. She revealed to the king Haman's clandestine plot to destroy the Jewish people.   The king had Haman hanged and then modified the decree that called for the destruction of the Jewish people. In this situation, fasting and prayer helped save thousands of people from destruction.

In the New Testament, Jesus Christ demonstrated the importance of fasting. Before he was to begin his ministry and select his apostles, he went into the wilderness to fast and pray. Luke records, *"And Jesus being full of the Holy Ghost returned from Jordan and was led by the Spirit into the wilderness...And in those days he did eat nothing...."*[80]

Jesus wanted to draw close to his Heavenly Father and to know his holy mind and will, so he went where he could be alone and spent his time fasting and praying. After the Savior completed his fast, the devil came to tempt him. But Jesus rebuked him with the words, *"Get thee behind me, Satan...."*[81]

As a result of fasting and prayer, the Savior was able to resist temptation and receive the revelation he needed to undertake the most difficult mission in the history of the world.

The Savior taught us that we should not fast to be seen of the world or to solicit the admiration or sympathy of the world. He said, *"Moreover when ye fast, be not, as the hypocrites, of a sad countenance: for they disfigure their faces, that they may appear unto men to fast. Verily I say unto you, they have their reward. But thou, when thou fastest, anoint thine head, and wash thy face; That thou appear not unto men to fast, but unto thy Father which is in secret: and thy Father which seeth in secret, shall reward thee openly."*[82]

How Long Should We Fast?

Although the Savior fasted for forty days, as did several of the prophets in the Old Testament, it is not wise for us to fast for long periods of time. Most of us are not able to take extended periods of time away from our jobs and/or caring for a family to fast and pray. However, we can fast for a day. This should provide sufficient time to allow us to focus on our petitions to our Father in Heaven and to demonstrate the sincerity and earnestness of our prayers.

Some people may feel the need to fast for longer periods of time to accommodate their needs and circumstances. This is a personal matter that is left to the discretion and wisdom of each person according to their situation.

If we begin our fast right after a meal and then fast until that same meal the next day, forgoing the two meals in between, we will have fasted for about twenty-four hours. And although fasting is appropriate on any day of the week, Sunday may be the best day since it is the Lord's day and the day when we should set aside the cares of the world to focus on the things of God.

I believe that fasting, like anything else, can be abused or overdone. If we develop the habit of fasting every week or several times a week, we are not exercising good judgment and could damage our health.

I have found that what works best for me is to fast when I have a special concern or I want to draw closer to my Father in Heaven. I also fast one day a month on a regular basis.

I don't believe anyone should be forced to fast against his or her will, nor should little children be compelled to fast. Fasting is of benefit only when it is a personal choice and is accompanied by prayer. Fasting without praying is just going hungry and serves little useful spiritual purpose.

People with delicate health and those who may suffer from diabetes or other illnesses, as well as mothers who are pregnant or nursing, should be very careful before deciding to participate in a fast. The

Lord knows our situation and understands if our circumstances preclude us from fasting.

Special Blessings from Fasting

About 700 BC, Isaiah the prophet talked about the fast. He said, *"Is not this the fast that I have chosen? To loose the bands of wickedness, to undo the heavy burdens, and to let the oppressed go free, and that ye break every yoke?"*[83] Here, the prophet tells us that fasting can help us become more righteous, overcome some of the heavy burdens we have to bear, resist temptation, and overcome addictive behavior.

Isaiah teaches us to look beyond just fasting and praying for our own family or extended family and to look to the needs of the poor. He said, *"Is it not to deal thy bread to the hungry, and that thou bring the poor that are cast out to thy house? When thou seest the naked, that thou cover him; and that thou hide not thyself from thine own flesh?"*[84] We are here counseled to combine tending to the needs of those who are poor with the fast.

There is an obvious connection in that we can give the cost of the food we are forgoing during our fast to the poor. Fasting also offers the blessing of empathy and understanding in that we may come to know, at least to a degree, what it is like to be hungry, a condition that afflicts hundreds of millions of people in the world today. If we donate to the poor the value of the food we have not eaten during our fast, or an even greater contribution if we are in a position to do so, our Heavenly Father will bless us greatly.

In fact, Isaiah cites a long list of the wonderful blessings our Father in Heaven offers his children if they fast and pray and give to the poor. He records, *"Then shall thy light break forth as the morning, and thine health shall spring forth speedily: and thy righteousness shall go before thee; the glory of the Lord shall be thy rereward. Then shalt thou call, and the Lord shall answer; thou shalt cry, and he shall say, Here I am. ... And if thou draw out thy soul to the hungry, and satisfy the afflicted soul; then shall thy light rise in obscurity, and thy darkness be as the noonday: And the Lord shall guide thee continually, and satisfy thy soul in drought, and make fat thy bones: and thou shalt be like a watered garden, and like a spring of water, whose waters fail not."*[85]

What a wonderful cornucopia of blessings our Father in Heaven promises us if we observe the fast. Then we will have the glory of the Lord to protect us, our Heavenly Father will hear and answer our prayers, our light will rise from obscurity, the power of God will guide us continually, and inspiration and wisdom will flow from us like a spring of water that never runs out.

Chapter Ten

Great People Who Drew Upon the Power of Heaven

———•———

*M*ore things are wrought by prayer
than this world dreams of.
Wherefore, let thy voice
Rise like a fountain for me night and day,
For what are men better than sheep or goats
That nourish a blind life within the brain,
If, knowing God, they lift not hands of prayer
Both for themselves and those who call them
friend?[86]

--Alfred, Lord Tennyson
"The Passing of Arthur"

It is not possible to number or to fully understand
the magnitude of blessings that have come to those

who utilize the power of prayer. If we were to assemble a list of people who could testify of how prayer has enriched their lives, the roster would be endless. Even so, the review of such a list would surely give us hope and increase our faith. What follows is a tiny sampling of some well-known people from history who believed in the power of prayer.

George Washington

George Washington, known as the father of the United States, was an unselfish man of great integrity. He served as the Commander in Chief of the Continental Army and the first president of the United States. He was greatly respected and honored by his colleagues and the people of this fledgling nation and was one of the most influential Founding Fathers of America.

When George Washington was eleven years old, his father died, and George was sent to live with his half-brother at Mount Vernon. His mother, Mary Ball Washington, advised him: "Remember that God is our only sure trust. To him, I commend you . . . My son, neglect not the duty of secret prayer." These words that encouraged him to trust in God and to pray sank deep into his heart and became a standard by which he would live the rest of his life.

"When the First Continental Congress convened in 1774 and Thomas Jefferson called for a prayer to be offered, the Founders, each of them, in faith and humility bowed before their Maker. One delegate knelt. Bishop White, who was present, says that the kneeling man was George Washington." [87]

In spite of the fact that many people tried to attribute the incredible victories of the Revolutionary War to the leadership of George Washington, he always gave credit to God for his success. Today, if you were to travel to Valley Forge, you would find a large monument of George Washington, not posed in battle, but humbly kneeling to petition Heavenly Father for assistance.

Washington's prayer at Valley Forge illustrates his faith and humility, which he practiced throughout his life:

"Almighty and eternal Lord God, the great Creator of heaven and earth, and the God and Father of our Lord Jesus Christ; look down from heaven in pity and compassion upon me Thy servant, who humbly prostrate myself before Thee."

On May 1, 1777, news came that France was joining the war on the side of America. General Washington announced the news to his troops and then prayed:

"Almighty Father, if it is Thy holy will that we shall obtain a place and name among the nations of the earth, grant that we may be enabled to show our gratitude for Thy goodness, by our endeavors to fear and obey Thee. Bless us with wisdom in our councils, success in battle, and let all our victories be tempered with humanity. Endow, also, our enemies with enlightened minds, that they may become sensible of their injustice, and willing to restore our liberty and peace. Grant the petition of Thy servant for the sake of Him whom Thou hast called Thy beloved Son; nevertheless, not our will but Thine be done. Amen."[88]

Washington would later acknowledge that his petitions to heaven had been answered. During his first inaugural address in 1789, President George Washington, said:

"No people can be bound to acknowledge and adore the invisible hand, which conducts the affairs of men, more than the people of the United States. Every step by which they have advanced to the character of an independent nation seems to have been distinguished by some token of providential agency...It would be peculiarly improper to omit in this first official Act, my fervent supplications to that Almighty Being who rules over the Universe, who presides in the Councils of Nations, and whose providential aids can supply every human defect, that his benediction may consecrate to the liberties and happiness of the People of the United States, a Government instituted by themselves for these essential purposes. . ."[89]

George Washington had daily private prayers. Tim LaHaye gives evidence of this in his book, *Faith of Our Founding Fathers*, in which he references the experiences of Robert Lewis, who was Washington's private secretary. "Being a nephew of Washington, and his private secretary during the first part of his presidency, Mr. Lewis lived with him on terms of intimacy, and had the best opportunity for observing his habits. Mr. Lewis said that he had accidentally witnessed his private devotions in his library both morning and evening; that on those occasions he had seen him in a kneeling posture with a Bible open before him, and that he believed such to have been his daily practice."[90]

In his farewell address to the American people, September 19, 1796, George Washington urged that the citizens of the United States not forget about religion as he knew of its importance in his life and in establishing, building, and sustaining a nation.

> "Of all the dispositions and habits which lead to political prosperity, religion and morality are indispensable supports...Let us with caution indulge the supposition that morality can be maintained without religion."[91]

John Adams

John Adams was a very intelligent Harvard-educated lawyer who was a leader in the movement for independence and one of America's Founding Fathers. He served as the Vice President under George Washington and became the second President of the United States in 1797.

He was both a devout Christian and an independent thinker. "Prayer got him through his most difficult times, and he rebuked many of the 'enlightened' figures of his day who mocked Christianity."[92]

In his inaugural address of March 4, 1797, John Adams concluded with the following statement:

"And may that Being who is supreme over all, the Patron of Order, the Fountain of Justice, and the Protector in all ages of the world of virtuous liberty, continue His blessing upon this nation and its Government and give it all possible success and duration consistent with the ends of His providence."

During his presidency, Adams proclaimed a National Day of Fasting and Prayer, in which he stated the following:

"As the safety and prosperity of nations ultimately and essentially depend on the protection and blessing of Almighty God; and the national acknowledgment of this truth is not only an indispensable duty which the people owe to Him, but a duty whose natural influence is favorable to the promotion of that morality and piety, without which social happiness cannot exist, nor the blessings of a free government be enjoyed; and as this duty, at all times incumbent, is so especially in seasons of difficulty and of danger, when existing or threatening calamities, the just judgments of God against prevalent iniquity are a loud call to repentance and reformation; and as the United States of America are at present placed in a hazardous and afflictive situation, by the unfriendly disposition, conduct and demands of a foreign power. . . Under these considerations it has appeared to me that the duty of imploring the mercy and benediction of Heaven on our country, demands at this time a special attention from its inhabitants. I have therefore thought it fit to recommend, that Wednesday, the 9th day of May next be observed throughout the United States, as a day of Solemn Humiliation, Fasting and Prayer."[93]

Thomas Jefferson

Thomas Jefferson was considered by many to be one of the most brilliant men to ever occupy the White House. Few men did more to help shape this nation, as he dedicated most of his life to public service. He was not only the main author of the Declaration of Independence, but he also wrote the Virginia civil code, founded the state university of Virginia, devised the decimal system of coinage in dollars and cents, and amassed a large library which ultimately became the Library of Congress. Although he was primarily a statesman, he was also a skilled lawyer, writer, naturalist, musician, botanist, paleontologist, mathematician, farmer, and architect.

When President John F. Kennedy hosted a White House dinner honoring 49 Nobel Prize winners in 1962, he said, "I think this is the most extraordinary collection of talent, of human knowledge, that has ever been gathered together at the White House, with the possible exception of when Thomas Jefferson dined here alone."

This brilliant man did not depend totally on his own intellect, but had the wisdom to petition heaven to bring the power of God into his life. One example of his belief in prayer was demonstrated in 1774 while he was serving in the Virginia Assembly, where he introduced a resolution calling for a Day of Fasting and Prayer.

When he gave his second inaugural address on March 4, 1801, it was clear that he also wanted the people of the country to petition the Almighty for wisdom to help him in his presidency. He said,

"I shall need, too, the favor of that Being in whose hands we are, who led our fathers, as Israel of old, from their native land and planted them in a country flowing with all the necessaries and comforts of life; who has covered our infancy with His providence and our riper years with His wisdom and power, and to whose goodness I ask you to join in supplication with me that He will enlighten the mind of your servants, guide their councils and prosper their measures, that whatsoever they do shall result in your good, and shall secure to you the peace, friendship, and approbation of all nations."[94]

"He [Jefferson] like Washington and many other patriots, believed that God had... blessed them in their infant government as well as in their riper years. He prayed that 'that Infinite Power which rules the destinies of the Universe lead our councils to what is best and give them favorable issue for our peace and prosperity.'"[95]

John Quincy Adams

John Quincy Adams, sixth president of the United States of America, was a very religious man and a devout Christian. He had a devout mother who helped instill within him a strong faith in God. He attended church regularly throughout his life, read the Bible faithfully, and praised its teachings.

When it was feared that Christian influence was waning in New England, he prepared a lecture on Truth, which he delivered in many places. The premise was:

"A man to be a Christian must believe in God, in the Bible, in the Divinity of the Savior's mission, and in a future state of rewards and punishments."

"Adams wrote a series of letters to his son on "The Bible and its Teachings," which were published in the New York Tribune, in which he stated:

"I have myself for many years made it a practice to read through the Bible once every year. I have always endeavored to read it with the same spirit and temper of mind which I now recommend to you; that is, with the intention and desire that it contribute to my advancement in wisdom and virtue ... My custom is, to read four or five chapters every morning, immediately after rising from my bed. It employs about an hour of my time, and seems to me the most suitable manner of beginning the day." [96]

John Quincy Adams, in 1825, was the first president to directly quote from the Bible in his inaugural address. He concluded his address as follows:

"To the guidance of the legislative councils, to the assistance of the executive and subordinate departments, to the friendly cooperation of the respective State governments, to the candid and liberal support of the people so far as it may be deserved by honest industry and zeal, I shall look for whatever success may attend my public service; and knowing that "except the Lord keep the city the watchman waketh but in vain," with fervent supplications for His favor, to His overruling providence I commit with humble but fearless confidence my own fate and the future destinies of my country."[97]

John Quincy Adams strongly valued prayer and insisted frequently that God directs history and guides our lives. His faith in prayer can be observed in his own words:

"For I believe there is a god who heareth prayer, and that honest prayers to him will not be in vain."[98]

Abraham Lincoln

Abraham Lincoln was a man known for his integrity and was beloved by the people. Ralph Waldo Emerson said;

"Abraham Lincoln ... was at home and welcome with the humblest, and had a spirit and a practical vein in the times of terror that commanded the admiration of the wisest. His heart was as great as the world, but there was no room in it to hold the memory of a wrong."[99]

John Hay, Lincoln's private secretary, once said, "Lincoln, with all his foibles, is the greatest character since Christ." And Dr. Theodore Cuyler said, "Lincoln is the best loved man that ever trod this continent."[100]

In his farewell speech to his friends, just before leaving for Washington D.C. to begin his presidency, Lincoln showed his faith in and dependence on God:

> "I go to assume a task more difficult than that which devolved upon any other man since the days of Washington. He never would have succeeded except for the aid of Divine Providence, upon which he at all times relied. I feel that I cannot succeed without the same Divine blessing which sustained him; and on the same Almighty Being I place my reliance for support. And I hope you, my friends, will all pray that I may receive that Divine assistance without which I cannot succeed, but with which success is certain. Again I bid you an affectionate farewell."[101]

Abraham Lincoln had a strong belief in God and a powerful conviction of prayer. Many of Lincoln's presidential speeches are superb examples of a man seeking God. Below is a portion of one of Lincoln's many proclamations, as president, for a national day of fasting and prayer:

> "It is the duty of nations as well as of men to own their dependence upon the overruling power of

God, and to confess their sins and transgressions in humble sorrow, yet with assured hope that genuine repentance will lead to mercy and pardon, and to recognize the sublime truth, announced in Holy Scripture, and proven by all history, that those nations only are blessed whose God is the Lord... We have been the recipients of the choicest bounties of Heaven; we have been preserved these many years in peace and prosperity; we have grown in numbers, wealth and power as no other nation has ever grown. But we have forgotten God. We have forgotten the gracious hand which has preserved us in peace and multiplied and enriched and strengthened us, and we have vainly imagined, in the deceitfulness of our hearts, that all these blessings were produced by some superior wisdom and virtue of our own. Intoxicated with unbroken success, we have become too self-sufficient to feel the necessity of redeeming and preserving grace, too proud to pray to the God that made us. It behooves us, then, to humble ourselves before the offended power, to confess our national sins and to pray for clemency and forgiveness."[102]

The following statement made to General Dan Sickles, a participant in the battle of Gettysburg, also demonstrates Lincoln's humble, unquestioned dependence on our Father in Heaven:

"Well, I will tell you how it was. In the pinch of your campaign up there, when everybody seemed panic-stricken and nobody could tell what was going to happen, oppressed by the gravity of our affairs, I went to my room one day and locked the door and got down on my knees before Almighty God and prayed to him mightily for victory at Gettysburg. I told Him that this war was His, and our cause His cause, but we could not stand another Fredericksburg or Chancellorville. Then and there I made a solemn vow to Almighty God that if He would stand by our boys at Gettysburg, I would stand by Him, and He did stand by you boys, and I will stand by Him. And after that, I don't know how it was, and I cannot explain it, soon a sweet comfort crept into my soul. The feeling came that God had taken the whole business into His own hands, and that things would go right at Gettysburg, and that is why I had no fears about you."[103]

It is interesting to note that within about three months from the time that Lincoln had asked the nation to fast and pray on March 30, 1863, the Union Army was victorious at Gettysburg, which became the turning point in the Civil War. Later that same year, Abraham Lincoln issued a proclamation calling for a national day of thanksgiving and prayer. The final paragraph of that proclamation, which follows, shows Lincoln's gratitude to Heavenly Father and his strong belief in prayer.

"I do therefore invite my fellow citizens in every part of the United States, and also those who are at sea and those who are sojourning in foreign lands, to set apart and observe the last Thursday of November next, as a day of Thanksgiving and

Praise to our beneficent Father who dwelleth in the Heavens. And I recommend to them that while offering up the ascriptions justly due to Him for such singular deliverances and blessings, they do also, with humble penitence for our national perverseness and disobedience, commend to His tender care all those who have become widows, orphans, mourners or sufferers in the lamentable civil strife in which we are unavoidably engaged, and fervently implore the interposition of the Almighty Hand to heal the wounds of the nation and to restore it as soon as may be consistent with the Divine purposes to the full enjoyment of peace, harmony, tranquility and Union."[104]

Benjamin Franklin

Benjamin Franklin was a scientist and an inventor. Some of his inventions include bifocal glasses, the Franklin stove, the lightning rod, and the odometer. He was a statesman, a printer, a philosopher, a musician, and an economist. He developed America's first circulating library, and a postal system for Philadelphia. This ingenious man was also a skilled diplomat, ambassador, and statesman who helped in drafting both the Declaration of Independence and the Constitution. He was one of the Founding Fathers and one of America's greatest citizens.

Benjamin Franklin prepared and read the following "Address on Prayer" before the Constitutional Convention:

"Mr. President,

"The small progress we have made after four or five weeks' close attendance and continual reasonings with each other—our different sentiments on almost every question, several of the last producing as many noes as ayes—is, methinks, a melancholy proof of the imperfection of the human understanding . . . .

"In this situation of this assembly, groping as it were in the dark to find political truth, and scarce able to distinguish it when presented to us, how has it happened, sir, that we have not hitherto once thought of humbly applying to the Father of lights, to illuminate our understandings? In the beginning of the contest with Great Britain, when we were sensible of danger, we had daily prayer in this room for the divine protection. Our prayers, sir, were heard; and they were graciously answered . . . .

"I have lived, sir, a long time; and, the longer I live, the more convincing proofs I see of this truth, – that God governs in the affairs of men. And, if a sparrow cannot fall to the ground without His notice, is it probable that an empire can rise without His aid? We have been assured, sir, in the sacred writings that "except the Lord build the house they labor in vain that build it." I firmly believe this; and I also believe that without His concurring aid we shall succeed in this political building no better than the builders of Babel. We shall be divided by our little partial local interests, our projects will be confounded, and we ourselves shall become a reproach and byword to future ages. And, what is worse, mankind may hereafter from this unfortunate instance despair of establishing governments by human wisdom, and leave it to chance, war and conquest.

"I therefore beg leave to move that henceforth prayers imploring the assistance of Heaven, and its blessings on our deliberations, be held in this Assembly every morning before we proceed to business..."[105]

Ralph Waldo Emerson

Ralph Waldo Emerson found God after the death of his young wife. At this painful time in his life, rather than falling into darkness and despair, he turned to prayer and introspection. It was during this period of spiritual awakening that he wrote the following:

> "Our goodness is so low that it scarce seems to approximate to truth and our knowledge so scanty that it does not approximate to virtue. But in God they are one. He is perfectly wise because he is perfectly good; and perfectly good because he is perfectly wise... The only way to stand is to cling to the Rock. Keep the soul always turned to God. Nothing so vast but feel that he contains it. Let nothing be so real or pure or grand as He is. If your idea of him is dim or perplexed pray and think and act more. It is the education of the soul."[106]

In the year 1838, Ralph Waldo Emerson delivered an address before the senior class of the Divinity School at Cambridge University in England to stimulate the thinking of the students. He challenged them to understand and teach that the God of heaven to whom we pray actually exists and is not the God of yesteryear; he lives! He said:

> "It is the office of a true teacher to show us that God is, not was; that He speaketh, not spake. ...Men have come to speak of ...revelation as somewhat long ago given and done, as if God were dead."[107]

C.S. Lewis

C.S. Lewis is said to be one of the greatest and most brilliant literary minds of the last century. Lewis converted from Atheism to Christianity during the course of his life, and proceeded to write many works analyzing and defending Christianity. Included in his writings are the following thoughts on prayer:

> "If we were perfected, prayer would not be a duty, it would be delight."[108]

> "We must lay before Him what is in us, not what ought to be in us."[109]

> "On a day of traveling with, perhaps, some ghastly meeting at the end of it I'd rather pray sitting in a crowded train than put it off till midnight when one reaches a hotel bedroom with aching head and dry throat and one's mind partly in a stupor and partly in a whirl."[110]

> "I have seen many striking answers to prayer and more than one that I thought miraculous."[111]

> "Can we believe that God ever really modifies His action in response to the suggestions of men? For

infinite wisdom does not need telling what is best, and infinite goodness needs no urging to do it. But neither does God need any of those things that are done by finite agents, whether living or inanimate.

"He could, if He chose, repair our bodies miraculously without food; or give us food without the aid of farmers, bakers, and butchers, or knowledge without the aid of learned men; or convert the heathen without missionaries. Instead, He allows soils and weather and animals and the muscles, minds, and wills of men to cooperate in the execution of His will.

"It is not really stranger, nor less strange, that my prayers should affect the course of events than that my other actions should do so. They have not advised or changed God's mind—that is, His overall purpose. But that purpose will be realized in different ways according to the actions, including the prayers, of His creatures."[112]

C. S. Lewis expressed his feelings about prayer in the following quotation he used from a 20th century theologian named William Barclay:

"Prayer is not a way of making use of God; prayer is a way of offering ourselves to God in order that He should be able to make use of us. It may be that one of our great faults in prayer is that we talk too much and listen too little. When prayer is at its highest we wait in silence for God's voice to us; we linger in His presence for His peace and His power to flow over us and around us; we lean back in His everlasting arms and feel the serenity of perfect security in Him..." [113]

Sir Isaac Newton

One of the greatest scientists who ever lived, Sir Isaac Newton made significant contributions in the areas of astronomy, optics, and physics and is credited with developing the mathematical discipline known as calculus. He also invented the reflecting telescope and discovered the law of universal gravitation and the three laws of motion.

He was wise enough to value both science and religion, and as such, he wrote papers refuting atheism and defending Christianity and the Bible. He said,

"I have a fundamental belief in the Bible as the Word of God, written by men who were inspired. I study the Bible daily."[114]

He had a strong belief that God was the supreme Creator in charge of the universe, evidence of which can be found in his Principia:

"The most beautiful system of the sun, planets, and comets, could only proceed from the counsel and dominion of an intelligent and powerful Being."[115]

The following anecdote is also attributed to Newton:

"One time an atheist friend of Newton's came over and saw this scale model of the solar system that Newton had. He remarked at how beautiful it was and asked who made it. Newton nonchalantly replied that no one did; it just made itself. The atheist asked again, got the same answer, and started to get angry. Newton replied, 'If you cannot believe something as simple as this model cannot make itself, how can you believe the heavens made themselves? This thing—an orrery, a scale model of the solar system, is but a puny imitation of a much grander system whose laws you know, and I am not able to convince you that this mere toy is without a designer and maker; yet you, as an atheist, profess to believe that the great original from which the design is taken has come into being without either designer or maker! Now tell me by what sort of reasoning do you reach such an incongruous conclusion?' "

Sir Isaac Newton had a strong belief in prayer and always gave credit to God for his success. He said,

> "And as for the Christian worship, we are authorized in scripture to give glory and honour to God the Father, because he hath created all things, and to the Lamb of God, because he hath redeemed us with his blood and is our Lord, and to direct our prayers to God the Father in the name of Christ ...."[116]

Regarding his monumental scientific discoveries, Newton said,

> "All my discoveries have been made in an answer to prayer."[117]

God Answers Prayers

I know not by what method rare,
But this I know, God answers prayer.
I know that He has given His Word,
Which tells me prayer is always heard.
And will be answered, soon or late.
And so I pray and calmly wait.
I know not if the blessing sought,
Will come in just the way I thought;
But leave my prayer with Him alone
Whose will is wiser than my own.
Assured that He will grant my quest,
Or give some answer far more blessed.
(author unknown)

Chapter Eleven

Another Testimony of the Power of Prayer

———•·•———

I express my thanks to the many people who have shared their inspiring, uplifting, and wonderful experiences, and add my testimony to theirs of the efficacy of prayer. Prayer has completely changed and enriched my life. It is the greatest and most underutilized resource in the universe.

Our kind and generous Heavenly Father has opened the windows of heaven and showered upon me so many incredible blessings. He has answered thousands of my petitions that have opened incredible windows of opportunity and helped me to accomplish tasks I could never have achieved without his assistance.

He has blessed me when in the valley of despair, brought peace to my soul while waiting to go into the operating room, comfort during times of tremendous pain, and joy to my heart as I have felt of his love and concern. These answers to my prayers are about his generosity, not about my worthiness.

I have absolute trust and confidence in our Father in Heaven and know that he only wants what is best for us. He is the one dependable, never-failing source of strength. His love is unconditional, and even when we do things that are not pleasing to him, he still loves us and cares about us.

When we come to recognize the power of our perfect Heavenly Father and our own inadequacies, we will want his divine assistance to help us through the trials and challenges of life. Then we will petition him for the wisdom to know what to pray for and ask him to grant our requests *only* if they are in accordance with his holy mind and will.

The greatest discovery of my life was learning that I am a child of a personal, compassionate Heavenly Father who loves us and will help us if we ask. And because of his love for us, he has given to us Jesus Christ to serve as our role model, teacher, and Savior. If we follow his teachings he will make it possible for us to live in an unending paradise one day that will make any hardships, trials, or pain we have had to endure in this life more than worth the sacrifice. If we will continue to pray to Heavenly Father and always remember the Savior, we will be given God's Spirit to serve as a moral compass that will help us make the correct choices in life and to give us great hope of the joy that will come to us in this life and in the world to come.

1. Psalm 147:4-5
2. NASA press release issued on the Hubble Website on February 15, 2004.
3. *The Complete Works of Ralph Waldo Emerson*, Volume VIII, "Letters and Social Aims" (1876).
4. Judges 6:15
5. Judges 7:12
6. John 3: 16
7. John 14: 6-9
8. John 5: 19-20
9. Hebrews 1: 3
10. Mark 10:14
11. Matthew 10:29-31
12. Mere Christianity 1943, p. 131
13. Psalms 8: 4-5
14. Genesis 1:26-27
15. Mark 12:29–30; see also Matthew 22:37–38; Deuteronomy 6:5
16. Matthew 7:7-11
17. Luke 21:36
18. Matthew 6:7
19. Ephesians 5:20
20. James 1:5
21. Matthew 6:8
22. Matthew 6:9
23. 1 Thessalonians 5:17-18
24. Matthew 21:22
25. Mark 14:36
26. John 14:6
27. John 16:23
28. Luke 11:9-10
29. Mark 2:16-17
30. Luke 15:10
31. Luke 15:20
32. Acts 10:34
33. 1 Kings 19:12
34. Psalms 46:10
35. Ephesians 4:27
36. Ephesians 6:11
37. James 4:7-8

[38] Galatians 5:22-23
[39] James 3: 17-18
[40] Isaiah 55:8
[41] Luke 22:42
[42] Matthew 6:10
[43] Matthew 6:9, emphasis added
[44] Hebrews 11:6 emphasis added
[45] Mark 11:24, emphasis added
[46] James 1:6, emphasis added
[47] *Hamlet, Prince of Denmark*, Act 3, Scene 3
[48] *The Adventures of Huckleberry Finn, New York and Scarborough, Ontario: New American Library, 1959, pp. 208-9.*
[49] Matthew 6:7
[50] Ecclesiastes 5: 2-3
[51] 1 John 5:14, emphasis added
[52] John 8:28
[53] Luke 22:44, emphasis added
[54] Luke 22: 42, emphasis added
[55] Phillips Brooks, Going Up to Jerusalem, In Visions and Tasks, p. 330
[56] 1 Corinthians 10:13
[57] Mark 6: 40-45
[58] The Roman system of watches divided the night into four, three hours watches, beginning at 6:00 p.m.
[59] Matthew 14: 27; Mark 6:50
[60] C. H. Spurgeon, Gleanings Among the Sheaves, 2d ed. (New York: Sheldon, 1869.) The Use of Trials.
[61] 2 Corinthians 11: 24-27
[62] 2 Corinthians 12:7-8
[63] 2 Corinthians 12:9
[64] 2 Corinthians 12: 10, emphasis added
[65] Daniel 3 16-18
[66] Daniel 3: 19
[67] Daniel 3: 20
[68] Daniel 3:29
[69] (C. S. Lewis, Mere Christianity, New York: Simon & Schuster, 1996 p. 176.)

[70] A Tale of Two Cities by Charles Dickens, Oxford University Press, 1949, p.1.

[71] 2 Timothy 3:1-4

[72] Matthew 24: 6-7, 12

[73] 2 Timothy 1:7

[74] Ephesians 6: 13, 18

[75] Proverbs 22:6

[76] Isaiah 54:13

[77] Matthew 18:20

[78] Exodus 34:28, Deuteronomy 9:9 1 Kings 19:8

[79] Esther 4:16, emphasis added

[80] Luke 4:1-2

[81] Luke 4:8

[82] Matthew 6:16-18

[83] Isaiah 58:6

[84] Isaiah 58: 7

[85] Isaiah 58: 8-11

[86] The Passing of Arthur, Idylls of the King, 1869.

[87] Schroeder-Lossing. *Life and Times of Washington.* 2:658.

[88] *Prayers Suitable for the Times in Which We Live.* Charleston: Evans & Cogswell, No. 3 Board Street 1861.

[89] *George Washington's First Inaugural Address,* 30 April 1789, New York City.

[90] LaHaye, Tim. *Faith of Our Founding Fathers.* (Brentwood, Tennessee: Wolgemuth & Hyatt, Publishers, Inc.,   1987), p. 103.

[91] George Washington: Farewell Address, in William Benton, pub., *The Annals of America,* 21 vols. (1968–87), 3:612.

[92] Moreno, Paul: Book Review of *John Adams* by David McCullough.

[93] The Phenix/Windam Herald, April 12, 1798.

[94] Thomas Jefferson's Second Inaugural Address, March 4, 1805.

[95] Petersen, Mark. *The Great Prologue*, p.94.

[96] (Adapted from American Christian Rulers, Rev. Edward J. Gidding (New York: Bromfield & Company, 1890) pp. 6-13.)

[97] John Quincy Adams Inaugural Address, March 4, 1825.

[98] Quincy Unitarian Church Website, http://www.uuquincy.org/projects/stamps/4johnquincy.htm

[99] The Works of Ralph Waldo Emerson, Greatness, Letters and
      Social Aims (1876).
[100] McClure, Colonel Alexander K. *Lincoln's Yarns and Stories.*
[101] Gross, Anthony. *The Wit and Wisdom of Abraham Lincoln.*
      1992, p.73.
[102] Abraham Lincoln's Proclamation for a National Day of
      Humiliation, Fasting, and Prayer. Washington, D.C. March
      30, 1863.
[103] Hill, John Wesley. *Abraham Lincoln—Man of God.* New
      York: G. P. Putnam's Sons, 1927, pp. 339–40.
[104] Abraham Lincoln issued The Thanksgiving Proclamation on
      October 3, 1863 in Washington, D.C.
[105] Madison, James. *Journal of the Federal Convention, Volume
      1*, p. 259-260.
[106] Gilman, William H. and Alfred R. Ferguson, editors. *The
      Journals and Miscellaneous Notebooks of Ralph Waldo
      Emerson*, Volume III, 1826-1832. Belknap Press of Harvard
      University, Cambridge: 1963.
[107] Ralph Waldo Emerson *The Complete Works of Ralph Waldo
      Emerson*, pp. 37-45.
[108] Letters to Malcolm: Chiefly on Prayer, chapter 21, p.114
[109] Letters to Malcolm: Chiefly on Prayer, chapter 4, p.22
[110] Letters to Malcolm: Chiefly on Prayer, chapter 3 pp. 16-17
[111] The World's Last Night and Other Essays, The Efficacy of
      Prayer 1959, pp.10-11
[112] Lewis, C.S. "Can Prayer Change God's Mind?" *The Efficacy
      of Prayer.*
[113] Barclay, William. *The Plain Man's Book of Prayers*,
      Introduction; quoted by Lewis on August 5, 2000, Feast of
      Oswald, King of Northumbria, Martyr, 642.
[114] Tiner, J.H. *Isaac Newton—Inventor, Scientist and Teacher.*
      Mott Media, Milford (Michigan): 1975.
[115] Mathematical Principles of Natural Philosophy, The System of
      the World General Scholium.
[116] McLachlan, H., *Sir Isaac Newton: Theological Manuscripts.*
      Liverpool: 1950, pp. 29-35.
[117] Coppedge, David F. *The World's Greatest Creation Scientists
      from Y1K to Y2K*. David F. Coppedge, Master Plan Productions,
      2000.